"One of today's most distinguished writers on language and writing style—a freaking genius-god in the writing world."

—Jessica Page Morrell, Powell's Books Blog

"Have you used the word 'great' or 'fantastic' or 'awesome' in the last week? Ha! I thought so. Everyone has. And it's getting really really tiresome. In your hands lies a new way of life. Word-adroit Art Plotnik has compiled a collection of hundreds of juicy alternatives to your three favorite superlatives. A feloniously fun bedtime browsing treat, *Better Than Great* is also an unimpeachably useful daytime reference work. I can't believe I ever got published without it. It is, in a word, ripsniptious! (P.S. Never lend this book to anyone. You will not get it back. That happened to me.)"

—Rosalie Maggio, author of *How to Say It*

"For those who find themselves at a loss for praise-worthy words, feel there's a paucity of acclamatory expressions, or believe we are numbed by the plethora of platitudes that pass for superlatives, Arthur Plotnik's new book is *better than great*; it is iridescently indispensable, a bare-knuckled barrel of berserkley fun words."

—Phil Cousineau, author of *Wordcatcher: An Odyssey into the World of Weird and Wonderful Words*

"Plotnik's 'acclamatory hoard' is every bit as entertaining as it is useful. And (to lift one phrase) that ain't exactly chopped herring, considering it gives this critic some 6,000 substitutes for feeble old 'amazing' and its ilk."

—Bruce Ingram, film and entertainment critic at Sun-Times Media/Pioneer Press

"Arthur Plotnik's *Better Than Great* is a bouquet of perfection, a feel-good, all-purpose A-list Angel Cake of big-league tips on how to turn your complimentary powers into blue chip, berserkely good, yowzwers of social and professional opportunity."

—Alan Kaufman, author of *Jew Boy,* a memoir, and editor of *The Outlaw Bible of American Poetry*

BETTER THAN THAN GREAT

Also by Arthur Plotnik

The Elements of Editing:
A Modern Guide for Editors and Journalists

The Man Behind the Quill: Jacob Shallus,
Calligrapher of the United States Constitution

The Elements of Authorship:
Unabashed Advice, Undiluted Experience,
and Unadulterated Inspiration
for Writers and Writers-to-Be

The Elements of Expression:
Putting Thoughts Into Words

The Urban Tree Book:
An Uncommon Field Guide for City and Town

Spunk & Bite: A Writer's Guide to Bold,
Contemporary Style

BETTER THAN GREAT

A PLENITUDINOUS COMPENDIUM of WALLOPINGLY FRESH SUPERLATIVES

BY ARTHUR PLOTNIK

V!VA
EDITIONS

Published in the United States by Viva Editions,
an imprint of Cleis Press, Inc.,
2246 Sixth Street, Berkeley, California 94710.

Printed in the United States.
Cover design: Scott Idleman/Blink
Text design: Frank Wiedemann
First Edition.
10 9 8 7 6 5 4 3 2 1

Trade paper ISBN: 978-1-57344-660-0
E-book ISBN: 978-1-57344-681-5

Library of Congress Cataloging-in-Publication Data

Plotnik, Arthur.
 Better than great : a plenitudinous compendium of wallopingly fresh superlatives / by Arthur Plotnik. -- 1st ed.
     p. cm.
 ISBN 978-1-57344-660-0 (pbk. : alk. paper)
 1. English language--Adjective--Dictionaries. 2. English language--Usage--Dictionaries. I. Title.
 PE1241.P56 2011
 423'.1--dc22
                              2010053409

To these superlative women:
Mary, Julia, Katya,
Sondra, Tara, Annabelle, Barbara

CONTENTS

INTRODUCTION

PRAISE CAN BE
GREATER THAN AMAZING

Not every human trait is a cause for celebration, but one of them cheers me mightily: our zest for praising and acclaiming things we consider worthy. We love to do it. In the course of civilization, we have praised and acclaimed our divinities, heroes, beauties, works of art, and just about every other source of wonder or delight.

Praise challenges us to reveal our passions and powers of expression. Deft praise encourages others to feel as we do, to share our enthusiasms. It rewards deserving objects of admiration. It persuades people to take certain actions. It sells things.

And so each day we try to express acclaim for exceptional things: a new sushi joint, vacation spot, comedy, sports hero, love interest. But the terms we use for emphasis—terms repeated over the centuries and replicated virally in this one—are now anything but exceptional.

Our words and phrases of acclaim are worn out, all but impotent. Even so, we find ourselves defaulting to such habitual choices as *good*, *great*, and *terrific*, or substituting the weary synonyms that tumble out of a thesaurus— *superb*, *marvelous*, *outstanding*, and the like.

Sensing that such terms fall short, we pile on the usual intensifiers: <u>So</u> great. <u>Really</u> nice. <u>Totally</u> cool. We draw from such stock figures of speech as "Not too shabby," or "Good as gold." We call on intonation—"It was soooo— [two-beat pause]—awesome"—and nonverbal signals like jacked thumbs. In writing, we inject steroidal italics, uppercase letters, and exclamation marks: "She looked *spectacular*." "That was GREAT!!!"

But for all these options, how convincing are we? We'd like to be stimulating in our acclaim, go beyond the clichés that hype everything from soft drinks to arthritis drugs. We want to call attention to the special or superior quality of Entity X and convey our enthusiasm for it. Yet we rarely communicate that X was more than yawningly great, rarely evoke more than a nod or a "huh!," rarely persuade someone to share our conviction and even act on it.

The devices we call upon are played out. Our superlatives—terms indicating high or utmost degree—have lost their power to alert or entice; to amuse, distinguish, or sell. Like most words that become the rage, they soon suffer from overuse and devaluation. Terms expected to describe miracles, epiphanies, and colossal wonderments are exhausted on assignments like these:

Try our *amazing* onion rings.

That my beer? *Awesome*.

It's a *fantastic* mattress. I had a *fabulous* sleep.

At a loss for words with clout, we turn to negative modifiers—terms saying what something is not. A number of such modifiers have maintained their force. *Ineffable*, for example, carries a sense of "unspeakably sacred" or of speech being silenced by emotion. But the overused *unbelievable*, *not to·be believed*, and *incredible* have become black holes, threatening to swallow the universe of English modifiers. *Unbelievable*, which might have been reserved to describe talking cows or a century of peace, has been picked clean in the service of everyday, believable phenomena. *Incredible* hot dogs. *Unbelievable* sheets.

If anything escapes the pull of these terms, it gets gobbled up by *indescribable*—a word so quickly invoked as to signal easy surrender, expressing nothing. "The moon was indescribable" projects the same picture in my mind as "the moon was whatever."

Struggling to animate these forceless words, speakers

deliver them with giddy theatrics. "It was just—I mean really. Just. Absolutely. Incredible," we say, jaw slack and head wagging like a string puppet's. And I'm not mocking anyone—it's our natural behavior. I've head-wagged a lifetime, yearning for more effective expression.

Continued on page xvi.

AMAZING: THE "IT" WORD

"'R. Kelly keeps doing amazing things,' he said, blowing out the 'amazing' as if it were a party horn."

—Dave Itzkoff,
New York Times, June 4, 2010

Oh, that word *amazing*—enforced by dropping one's mandible on the second syllable and stretching out the *MAYYY* sound until a listener seems convinced. "I just ate the most a*MAYYY*zing cupcake."

Perhaps because the word is so easily brayed, *amazing* became the It utterance of the millennium's first decade. Never were so many so amazed at so much that amounts to so little. If something didn't suck it was amazing. Businesses from home siding to nail salons took on the name, each pedestrian use pushing the word further from its Middle English association with mazes, those bewildering, labyrinthine paths and passages. "To amaze" then meant to bewilder, perplex, and confuse, and in later times to overwhelm with surprise or sudden wonder, to astonish greatly. A bit much to ask of a cupcake.

BOLSTERING THE VOCABULARY

What now? Must we abandon *great*, *amazing*, and other beloved but worn-out superlatives? I doubt if we could, so habitually do such standbys leap to the tongue. Besides, in our everyday yakking they serve well enough to mean "a cut above." But short of being belted out from a soundstage, these terms can no longer seize attention and persuade an audience that something differently great has arrived.

A better choice than shouting old superlatives would be to add fresh, engaging terms to our acclamatory hoard: our vocabulary of praise, approval, and acclaim. But doing so isn't easy. By and large, thesauruses turn up equally worn alternatives under each worn superlative. Arcane options (like *Dhaulagirian*, after a soaring Nepalese mountain) have interesting but limited uses. Popular slang gets old in a wink, though it often enjoys a retro vogue.

One way to build a supply of uncommon superlatives would be to pore through several lexicons—hundreds of thousands of words and expressions—for new, under-used, recyclable, intensifiable, and tweakable candidates. And then do the recycling, intensifying, and tweaking to come up with a body of suggestions. Only a word-wonk would leap at such a task.

And, ahem, here I am. At your service.

Motivated partly by my ongoing interests in expressiveness and partly to ease my own addiction to *amazing* and its ilk, I have winnowed and shaped some 6,000 suggested alternatives to stale superlatives. I offer you not only a plug-and-play source of words and phrases, but models that will trigger your own brainstorming, your own inventions and usages. (See "Make Your Own Spumescently Brilliant Superlatives," in the following section, How to Use This Book.)

YOU

In addressing "you," I am picturing someone who takes language seriously, even when using it to evoke giggles and gasps. You are a novelist or a reporter reaching for an emphatic way of saying *beautiful* or *big*. You are a critic enchanted by a new work, but last week you used *enchanting*, *haunting*, and *mesmerizing* for the hundredth times. You cover sports, and that last-second touchdown was too special to lump with the thousands you've called *unbelievable* or *huge*. You are a copywriter, a marketer, groping for a term to vault your product above all other *fabulous*, *fantastic*, *groundbreaking*, and *ultimate* ones. You are an impassioned blogger/texter, tweeter, skilled at punchy put-downs but stuck at a level of *supercool* and *mind-boggling* when it comes to brief acclaim. You are everyperson, wishing to excite others about the things exciting you, or looking to energize such everyday civilities as "Have a _____ trip."

All such serious language users will find ways to recharge their acclamatory powers in this compilation, although they won't all find apt terms in the same groupings. My suggestions range from the literary (*aureate*, *ascendant*, *numinous*) to the funky (*trill*, *mind-foozling*, *butt-puckering*). Some, like *I've-fallen-and-I-can't-get-up gorgeous*, are flat-out farcical, more suited to blogs than graveside eulogies. Other offerings might sound alien to one's personal style but natural in the mouths of created characters:

> "You are an ebullition of joy!" Lady Bertram told her bubbly young visitor.

> "I've seen plenty of lookers in my racket," said Malone, "but this kid was armor-piercingly beautiful."

The appropriateness of any term will be up to its user, factoring in context, audience, and personal tastes. But among my suggestions are plenty of conservative as well as far-out alternatives to worn-out terms. I ask only indulgence as you scan past suggestions that seem too far-fetched or silly for your purposes. Someone else might find them cold-cockingly cool.

MYSELF

In a career that has included magazine and book editing, journalism, reviewing, copy writing, public relations, and authorship of eight books, I've long wrestled with about every type of expressiveness worth the effort. And much of that effort has been trying to extol, acclaim, or hype something in an expressive way. Earlier books of mine, such as *The Elements of Expression* and *Spunk & Bite: A Writer's Guide to Bold, Contemporary Style*, prompted writers to be more exciting, more engaging when putting any thoughts into words. But one of the toughest notions to get across in fresh language is how extraordinarily good or great something is.

Does it say anything about the human condition that terms for the extraordinarily negative (counting slang terms) are staggeringly more abundant and powerful than those of positive acclaim? So much so that we borrow such terms as ironic modifiers of the good: "She is *wicked* fine." "That new car is *bad*." "The *illest* movie around." (See "Wicked Cool" category.)

Let it be known that I relish the language of defamation, insult, and condemnation as much as I do any lively expression (unless of course the maledictions are directed at me). After all, I live in Chicago, where knocking politicians, rival cities, and cross-towners is an art form. But there are also scores of good things to celebrate here, as in your home town. With this compilation I've attempted to even the score somewhat and expand, with gusto, the ways you and I might say "super!"

Arthur Plotnik

HOW TO USE THIS BOOK

TIPS FROM THE AUTHOR

Need a fresh superlative in a hurry? Allergic to instructions? Then simply dip into the most likely categories (see Table of Contents or Index) to find a term you like. Tweak any suggested term to your own style or purpose. Look up unfamiliar words before springing them on judgmental audiences. That's it. Enjoy.

But for word-adventurers who favor an overview to enrich a journey, or who like to know the rationale, options, possibilities, and limitations of a new language tool, I offer the following mini-manual.

ARRANGEMENT AND FEATURES

Categories of acclaim tend to be vague and overlapping. Does a term fall under "Great" or "Fabulous?" "Amazing" or "Awesome?" In organizing this book I might have started with several dozen such common terms and listed approximate synonyms under each. But the lists would have been arbitrary and repetitive. Instead I sorted out 15 categories proving workably distinct from one another:

* Great
* Sublime
* Physically Affecting
* Mentally, Emotionally, or Spiritually Affecting
* Beautiful
* Joy-Giving
* Large
* Exceptional
* Intense
* Delicious
* Trendy
* Cool
* Wicked Cool
* Forceful
* Challenging Belief or Expression

Under each I indicated major related areas to help guide users. (See the head of each category or Index).

When terms defied a single category, I repeated them under two or three of the most suitable ones. *Olympian*, for example, I placed under the headings "Great," "Large," and "Sublime." The majority of suggested terms, however, can be used beyond their given categories by means of phrase-tweaking or deft application to a particular context. I list *high-voltage* under "Forceful," but its force could be applied within "Delicious" (high-voltage peppers), "Beautiful" (high-voltage sunset), "Trendy" (high-voltage hot pants), and other categories.

I've offered a few thoughts at the head of each category, and within some categories you'll find special "sidebar" features and lists. For example, under "Exceptional" there's a listing of "Rare Gems to Dangle as Metaphors," as in "She's a *Neelanjali Ruby* among garnets." Under "Delicious" you'll find a list of some 75 positive wine qualities. In several categories, the heading "Vintage Gold" offers a selection of still-punchy superlatives from yesteryear.

The appendices include the list "Previously Owned but Still Running," featuring some 100 selected entertainment and literary terms from recent promotional copy. Here writers might find "good-enough" choices for a routine job. Also in the appendices: 50 acclamatory terms in textese; 26 eponymous superlatives and how to make more; using alliteration in acclaim; and a starter set of superlatives to help break old habits.

Here and there I've placed examples of inspired

acclaim quoted from literature, journalism, and other sources. May you find all these features, along with the lists, to be both-barrels mind-blasting as you rev up your powers of praise.

CHOOSING THE RIGHT SUPERLATIVES

Superlatives are—or should be—powerful terms, proclaiming superiority with persuasive force. As with all things potent, their mishandling can blow up in one's face, so to speak. How can a term of praise, approval, and acclaim misfire? In several ways, including inappropriateness, overkill, insincerity, and downright impotence.

In order to grab attention in a world of sensory overload, most terms of acclaim are exaggerations. A pile of french fries hardly makes us tremble in awe, yet we call it *awesome*, exaggerating for the sake of persuasion. But because *awesome* is so worn out, the exaggeration doesn't register; it needs an element of novelty to help it do so. Novelty gets attention. "The fries were *industrial-strength awesome*." "The ride was *shiver-me-timbers awesome*."

With novelty, however, one invites attention to how something was said, which brings its own hazards. Not only is the object of your praise judged, but your manner of praising it.

We judge exaggeration kindly in commercial hype, even welcome it. *Set-off-the-fireworks fabulous! Double gulp-worthy!* I offer cartloads of such playful suggestions. But other situations are more delicate, calling for exaggeration that is inventive, tasteful, and infrequent. Too many clever superlatives at once can make one too clever by half, as they say.

Choosing among terms in any thesaurus-type work requires one to consider scores of choices—some personally repellent, some seductive—until hitting on one with the best meaning, nuance, tone, and sound for the occasion. And again as with other thesauruses, choice will be guided by whether the term is to be spoken or written, used formally or informally, and targeted to a general or particular audience. Readers of a term have a chance to savor its wordplay, images, nuances, and other delights, whereas conversation favors brief, vivid expression. More complicated locutions can seem strained and affected or just fly over the heads of listeners. *Keel-over cool* might work for me in conversation, but a term like *Mausoleum-of-King-Mausolas magnificent*? I might use it in a blog, but I wouldn't try to mouth it.

I've tried to anticipate the widest variety of uses for my suggested terms, so if you don't find your apt term right away, keep looking. Look under different categories, use the Index to Subcategories, or tweak a near-appropriate suggestion to suit your own purpose and style. (See "Make Your Own," below.)

Finally, be cautious in using unfamiliar terms, especially in writing. I've provided mini-definitions for terms I consider generally unfamiliar or misunderstood, but I could hardly offer notes on their usage here. "Beneath her veil was a *juggernaut* of beauty" suggests an overwhelming force of beauty, but also a cruel and destructive one. Take care; look up meanings when it matters, and pronunciation if you plan to speak the term.

MAKE YOUR OWN SPUMESCENTLY BRILLIANT SUPERLATIVES

In creating this compilation of acclamatory terms or superlatives, I've combed through thesauruses, lexicons, and glossaries for two types of prizes: first, strong existing terms that are not yet worn out (e.g., *supernal*, *empyreal*); and second, words and phrases I might configure into fresh acclamatory formations (*amen-astonishing*, *a cut above perfect*).

Lexicon searching yields only so many single-word synonyms (*outstanding*, *stupendous*, etc.) of the common superlatives. To create more alternatives, one must use additional words to intensify the common superlatives in fresh ways. For example, *concussively* great intensifies "great" not only by adding a modifier, but by using a fresh and vivid one (unlike, say, the limp *really*).

Every such suggested construction offers an opportunity to make creative substitutions. Don't like *concussively*? Then substitute *berserkly* or *clamorously*, or whatever best fits your context.

To find fresh modifiers of degree or manner for almost any purpose, simply pick out strong terms listed under one of my headings and apply them as appropriate. For example, my *breath-abating* (under "Great") can become your *breath-abatingly suspenseful*. My *clangorously real* can become your *clangorously new*, and so on.

Although negative evaluation was outside my scope, it need not be outside yours in making use of this book. The same tweaking of my suggestions, as described above, can amplify or refresh your vocabulary of negative appraisal, as in *breath-abatingly stupid*.

Many of my inventions are sparked by common rhetorical devices (figures of speech). For example, I've used the adverb *criminally* to energize the worn adjective *beautiful* because of *criminal*'s paradoxical-yet-meaningful sense in this context, a rhetorical effect called oxymoron. A writer can think of dozens of other contrary adverbs that would animate *beautiful* or its synonyms: *heinously beautiful*; *laceratingly gorgeous*; *actionably handsome*, and so on. Under "Great," I offer a list of such oxymoronic adverbs as a springboard.

Below are examples of some of the devices I've used. They can serve as models for writers creating their own fresh terms of acclaim. Knowing the name of a rhetorical figure is less important than picking up its pattern, which can then be used in creating terms for particular contexts.

Hyperbole: *mind-incinerating*; *it puts your atoms in orbit*

Personification: *eats great for breakfast*; *reality on a toot*; *what great aspires to*

Litotes (understatement): *not exactly nothing*; *hardly insignificant*

Germanism: *lock-me-up-and-throw-away-the-key gorgeous*; *trim-sail-and-batten-down-the-hatches mind-blowing*

Metaphor: *a tarantella on the tongue*; *a fun house*; *mastodonic*; *Eldorado*

Enallage (shifting a word's normal grammatical role): *great served hot*; *an eruption of fabulous*; *a hangarful of happy*

Oxymoron: *damnably good*; *distressingly handsome*

Alliteration: *pillar-to-post perfect*; *card-carrying cool* (See Appendix 4, All-Out Applause for Acclamatory Alliterations.)

Irony (opposite meaning): *the illest*; *way sick*; *the baddest*

A NOTE ON PARTS OF SPEECH

Sometimes freshness and novelty call for extreme measures. Taking advantage of English-language flexibility, I have recruited, stretched, mixed, and matched various parts of speech to create this body of acclamatory terms. I have employed nouns and noun phrases, like *a Queen Elizabeth at full steam*, describing what something is or can be compared to. I have used textured adjectives such as *iridescent* and *mellifluous*. And I have certainly used adverbs—words or phrases that modify adjectives, verbs, and other parts of speech.

I use tons of adverbs, and to those who still believe the old saw that all adverbs are bad, I say, heed the enlightened language experts: Adverbs are bad when they serve no purpose, when they add nothing but excess baggage to what they would modify. Otherwise, they serve to specify the degree or manner of the named quality, yielding information that is interesting, intensifying, and sometimes fun.

I have tried to use adverbs that energize and sharpen otherwise feeble terms of acclaim. If some of them seem over the top, it is because acclaim often needs to be so to stand out. Consider these examples culled from recent journalism and literature (adverbs in italics).

kneebucklingly sweet
blissfully deranged
captivatingly strange
devastatingly reasonable
wittily intricate
lashingly funny
searingly gifted
blamelessly beautiful

And so, Acclaimers, love your adverbs. Love any part of speech, any figure of speech, any language device that blasts a *walk-off homer** to be cheered by thousands.

---

* See under "Great."

KEY TO SYMBOLS AND ABBREVIATIONS

( )　Parentheses enclose brief definitions where judged helpful, source language (in italics), and occasional notes.

>*tiene duende* (*Sp.*: has a magical, inspired charm)

>Tiggerish (*ref.*, Tigger of *Winnie the Pooh*: cheerful, irrepressible)

!　Terms followed by an exclamation mark are suggested alternatives (slang or otherwise) to such common interjections as *wow! holy cow! cool! terrific! dude!*

>butta!

>g-o-a-a-l!

>tight!

,　An underlined punctuation mark within a suggested phrase is part of that phrase:

>in a nutshell, perfect

,   A plain comma (without underline) is not part of the phrase. It sets off a suggested beginning to the phrase:
> anointed, the
> ballet of swans, lovely as a

__   An underlined word is meant to be emphasized in speech.
> bail <u>out</u>!

ref.   A reference to
> Turneresque (*ref.*, English painter Joseph
>   Turner's fluent, radiant landscapes)

/   Slash between words means "either-or":
> to the utmost/uttermost boundaries

—   An *em* dash precedes a source given credit for original wording.
> "unbodied joy" (—Percy Bysshe Shelley,
>   "To a Skylark")

SOURCES

Generally helpful reference materials are given in Selected Sources. When a source has been uniquely informative about a term, that source is also credited alongside the term with one of the following abbreviations:

UD—*The Urban Dictionary*, and urbandictionary.com

Par.—*The Concise New Partridge Dictionary of Slang*

WS—Word Spy

GEOGRAPHIC USAGE

UK—More common in parts of the United Kingdom

CAN—Canadian use

AUSTRAL—Mainly Australian use

SCOT—Scottish use

JAM—Jamaican-influenced

NZ—New Zealand use

IR—Ireland use

FOREIGN LANGUAGES

As a rule, the language source is given for terms in use by a number of English-speakers but not yet adopted or adapted as part of the English language, according to major English dictionaries. Example: *guapo* (*Sp.*: handsome). For such terms (here in italics) careful users are advised to determine proper forms for gender, number, etc., depending on what is modified. Source notes are given for some adapted terms.

Fr.—French
Ger.—German
I.—Italian
Jap.—Japanese
L.—Latin
Sp.—Spanish (including Mexican and Central and South American)
Yi.—Yiddish
Hin.—Hindi

QUOTATIONS

Brief quoted phrases sometimes appear in the lists with minimal citations. As a rule those from literature get quotation marks; casually delivered phrases are simply credited.

"thing of beauty, a" (—John Keats)
vertiginously good (—Dwight Garner: dizzyingly)

Occasional longer quotations illustrate usage of terms in a category. Only terms from the lists are italicized in the quotations. Citations provide information sufficient to identify the source.

> "Their [the Human Eye Band's] second full-length release continues their musical mission with more *mind-derailing* time changes, ...
> —Matthew Smith, www.hookorcrook.com,
> May 18, 2010

THE
SUPERLATIVES

GREAT

- Extremely good
- Prized
- In Excellent Shape
- Distinguished
- Of Worldly Perfection
- Rich in Virtues
- Smart

A TOUGH WORD TO BEAT

Toward the end of the 20th century, the venerable word *great* reigned as the default term for describing specialty. Used at all levels of speech, the term never seemed to exhaust itself, even within a sentence. Major events called for pile-ups, something like, "This great float honors one of the great gentlemen of the great State of California, and tomorrow two great teams will play what's expected to be a great game before the greatest fans in this great nation."

Today, if the word doesn't quite put listeners to sleep, neither does it wake them to the wonders of anything. Approaching some two billion appearances in a Web search, it certainly has lost whatever specialty it had. If two billion things are special, what's left to be ordinary? In conventional uses, *great* generates about one nanowatt of energy. Lately the word *amazing* has become slightly more energetic than *great*, but it, too, is accumulating usage numbers that suggest serious loss of clout.

The problem is that *great*, considered by itself, is still a great word, understandably employed for more than a thousand years for a range of uses detailed across two pages of *The Oxford English Dictionary*. Force comes from its very sound, starting with a growl (*gr*), which can be drawn out, followed by its long-*a* attention-getter, and concluding with an emphatic dental mute, the *t*. Quick and punchy, it serves as both adjective and noun ("one of the greats") and shifts easily to the adverb *greatly*.

The word's early meanings of "thick" and "coarse" suggest its relation to Old English *grytta* (coarse-ground meal). Even if its grit has been chewed to mush in overuse, it can still be freshened by novel intensifying devices. At least that is the rationale for including, among our alternatives to *great*, suggestions for intensifying this worthy old utterance: *a blitzkrieg of greatness, fist-pumpingly great, great served hot, greatness in high relief*, and *thwackingly great*, to name just five of dozens.

What will the next hot modifier be? Hard to say; such terms slide in and out of fashion, emerging from standard synonyms, street-slang favorites, and pop-star locutions. "You look *mah*velous," intoned comedian Billy Crystal, and suddenly everyone was intoning it. Even *tha shiznit* got its run after Snoop Doggy Dog rapped it, never mind its etymology. But the zing of any term fades after the first few thousand uses and even faster among youth subcultures. Campus superlatives such as *bonus, core, key*, or *summit*? So 20th century. The once-hot teen superlatives *phat* and *fetch*? So yesterday for teens (though still in play for the rest of us).

Fading or not, certain acclamatory terms—*great, amazing, brilliant, terrific*, and *wonderful* among them—continue to serve as what Stuart Berg Flexner described as "blurred words":

> "… used quickly and without much thought, almost as automatic responses, because they are easily available.… The words are not always precise, which is one reason we like them so much.… [We] avoid arguments and fine distinctions we would rather not make."
>
> —*Listening to America*

But Flexner notes that while the words are imprecise, "we do want them to be forceful." Unfortunately, wanting does not do the job. For serious word users, it is invention, experimentation, discovery, and open-mindedness that puts the *grrr* back in terms of acclaim.

TERMS

abiding

above par (in good spirits/health)

absurdly great

abundantly gifted

acclaimable

ace serve, an

aces high

across-the-board brilliant

actuating angel, an (motivating one's higher actions)

acutely brilliant

A-double-1

adroit

afflated (having a divine inspiration from within)

afflatus, an (breath of inspiration from divinity)

airborne and volant (wings extended)

A-list

all aces

all of a piece with perfection

all systems go-go

all there and then some

all wool and a yard wide

all-around excellent

all-bets-off best

all-fired (remarkable; also excessive)

alliance of virtues, an

all-star

all-time wowser, an

alpha

alphabet of talents, an

amalgam of virtues, an

angel cake

anointed

antithesis of so-so, the

apex, the

Aphrodite, an

apical (forming the highest point)

apogee, the (highest point, apex)

applaudable

apposite (strikingly appropriate)

Arch-of-Triumph-worthy

aristocratic

arrantly brilliant (utterly, immoderately)

arrived

artista!

astute

at full sail

at its peak

atop the troposphere (first layer of the atmosphere)

au fait (*Fr.*: completely informed, expert)

august (dignified, imposing, high-ranking)

automatic Phi Beta Kappa

awash in greatness

awash in virtue

bacon, the

badda bing!

bang brilliant (*UK*, extremely brilliant)

bang-on (*UK*, just right)

bang-up

bankable!

banner

banner-head stuff (headline across all columns)

"bare-knuckled bucket of does, a" (—Verizon phone ad, 2009; "does" as in "does it all")

barnburner, a (exciting idea, thing, or happening)

barry (*SCOT*, excellent)

beastly fine

beats-all-hollow, the

beauteous maximus, a (phony Latin for something excellent)

bell-ringer, the

belta (*UK*, regional dialect; *US slang*: excellent)

benchmark, a

benison, a (blessing, benediction)

berserkly great

best bang for the click

best by six and a half lengths

best by ten furlongs (horse racing measure)

beyond finessed

Big Momma's baby

big-bang phenomenal

Big-Board winner (New York Stock Exchange)

big-league

big-ticket

bingo!

bis! bis! (a continental "encore!")

bizarrely great

black-belt

blackjack!

blastoff, a

blazoned with honors

blinder, a (*UK*, something dazzlingly good)

blindingly (dazzlingly)
blitzkrieg of greatness, a
block-rockin' (sensational)
blowout winner, a
blue peter hoisted (ready to sail)
blue blood, a
blue-book elegant
blue-chip
blue-ribbon
board-approved
body by Gdansk (shipyard city)
body by Peterbilt (truck maker)
bolt upright
bonanza, a
bone-brilliant
bone-crushingly great
bonny (excellent; also attractive)
booming
boomingly great
booted and spurred
bosses! (as in "it rules!")
bountifully good
bouquet of perfection, a
box seat, a
Brahmin (of social or cultural
    elite; high-priestly)
brainiac, a (smart person)
bran new (SCOT)
brass ring, the
bravo!

bravura
braw (SCOT, fine, good)
brazenly good
breadwinning
bright-eyed
brilliance unfurled
brilliant
brilliant in high relief
brilliantly dexterous
buckaroo, a (macho cowboy-like)
bueno (Sp.: good)
bull's-eye
bull-market
bullpen ace, the
bulls are running, the (stocks
    rising)
bumper crop, a
bung up and bilge free (ref., wine
    cask corked and above bilge
    level on ship)
butta! (butter)
buzz, the
buzzer play, a
calls the shots (as in "it rules")
canny
canonical (part of the approved
    core values or rules)
capacious greatness, a
capital
capital atop the pillar of perfec-

tion, the
capper, the
capping
capstone, the
captain, Team Terrific
caressably great
carved up (having muscular
   definition)
cash cow, a
cash money!
cat's nut, the (see "When the
   Bee's Knees Need Replace-
   ment" under "Trendy")
caution: greatness crossing
celestial tantara, a (fanfare, as on
   a horn)
centered (having self-confidence,
   stability, equilibrium)
cerebral
charitable
cheese, the
chef d'oeuvre, a (masterpiece)
chimingly great
chinchilla
chiseled in history
choccy! (as in chocolate)
choiceamundo
choice
chosen, the
circuit clout, a (home run)

clairvoyantly clued-in
clangorously great
classic cachet, a
classy
clean bill of perfection, a
clean sweep, a
cleans house (wins at betting)
cleans your clock
clean-up hitter, a (ref., key batter
   in baseball)
clear-eyed
clearheaded
clever in spades
clincher, the (act bringing
   closure, like a knockout
   punch)
cloaked in the mantle of greatness
clockwork-perfect
cloudburst of great, a
clued up/in (informed)
cluey (AUSTRAL, wise)
coin of the realm
cold cash
collectible, a
commanding
commendable
commodious greatness, a
complete package, the
concinnity, a (harmonious,

elegant arrangement of parts)

concinnous (elegant, harmoniously assembled)

consummate (lacking nothing)

convocation of eagles, majestic as a

cookin'

cordon bleu, a (blue ribbon; distinguished)

cork-popping

cornerstone, the

cosmic clangor, a

couched in splendor

could fart *The Barber of Seville*

could fetch water in a sieve

could harvest figs from thistles

could harvest grapes from thorns

coup de maître (*Fr.*: masterstroke)

cowabunga! (victory!)

cowing marvelous (*UK*)

crack (*UK*)

cracking (*UK*)

crash hot (*AUSTRAL*, excellent)

crazy great

crazy talented

creamy

crème de la crème, the

cropped and pruned to perfection

cross-court winner, a (pointscoring tennis play)

crown jewel, the

crowning

cultured

curtain-raiser to a golden age, the

curve-breaker, a

cushty (*UK*, excellent)

cut above perfect, a

cuts it cold

cutting (*UK*, excellent)

cynosure for all times, a (guiding star)

cynosure, a (focal point of admiration)

da-dah!/ta-dum! (a fanfare)

daedal (skillful, ingenious)

Dalai Lama-Mother Superior-Chief Rabbi approved

DAP (dead-ass perfect)

dead ahead

dead on target

deadly good

deal of two lifetimes, the

deathlessly brilliant

decrees! (as in "it rules!")

defiantly great

defining measure, the

deft

delivers the coup de grâce
(finishing stroke or blow)
deluxe
discerning
discourse in perfection, a
distingué/distinguée (having an
air of distinction)

drive-by genius, a
driving force, the
drum major for peace/justice/
righteousness, a (—Martin
Luther King, 1968)
droolworthy
dyno

"[T]hey're loaded with *droolworthy* features like turn-by-turn GPS instructions...."
—David Pogue, *New York Times*, June 23, 2010

---

distinguished
diva, a
dollop of perfection, a
dommo, a (*ref.*, board sports: a
dominating performer)
do-right citizen, a (righteous
person)
double-distilled
double-eagle, a (a hole in three
under par, golf)
double-rainbow brilliant
down the pipe
down-to-the-ground perfect
downtown
drained! (putt made, golf)

earthshaking
earth-shattering
easy street
eats great for breakfast
eats your lunch
ebulliently great
eclipsing
education in excellence, an
élan vital itself (organism's
creative force of growth and
adaptive change)
elder-statesmanly
Eldorado!
elegant (cleanly effective, as in an
elegant solution)

elevated

elite

embarrassed by its greatness

embossable in gold

eminent

emperor's choice, an

encore!

end-all of all end-alls, the

end-of-the-rainbow jackpot, the

endowed with greatness

enduringly fine

enduringly great

engraved on the roster of greatness

enlightenment, an

ennobled

ennobling

epicentral (at the focal point of activity)

epiphany, an (revelation)

epochal/epoch-making (momentous, as if to inaugurate a new epoch)

erudite

esteemed

estimable

euphoriant (inducing or an inducer of euphoria)

euphorigenic (yielding feeling of well-being)

eureka! moment, a

evincingly superior (demonstrably)

exalted

"A really strong woman accepts the war she went through and is *ennobled* by her scars."
—Carly Simon, Web posting, 2007

---

enriching

ensconced in greatness

enshrined in memory

enviable

epic

excellence distilled

excellence encapsulated

excellence pure and simple

executive-level

exemplar for the ages, an

exemplary
exponentially great
exquisite
extollable
fabled
fallen from the clouds
far-famed
Fat City
fat of the bat, the (*ref.*, best
    hitting area of baseball bat)
fat!
faultless
fifty-carat
fine tuned
finger-licking fabulous
fino
fire-god brilliant
firing on all cylinders
fist-pumping perfect
fist-pumpingly perfect
Fitness City
five of a kind (formidable hand
    in poker)
five-star
flagship of the line, the
flat-out phenomenal
flawless
flesh-and-blood priceless
flies in the face of mediocrity
found money

four aces (high poker hand)
four-bagger, a (home run, base-
    ball)
four-star
frabjous/most frabjous (—Lewis
    Carroll, *Through the Looking
    Glass*: fair, fabulous, and
    joyous)
freakin' freaky great
freestone-peachy
freethinking
front runner, the
front-page
frothingly great
fructuous (productive, fertile,
    profitable)
full-bore
full-turn fist-pumper, a (*ref.*,
    whirling gesture of triumph,
    athletics)
fusillade of brilliance, a
gala
galaxy-class
gallant (courageous, courteous)
game-changer, a
game-set-match (tennis victory)
game-winner, a
garden party, a
garlanded in virtue
geared for greatness

gelt (money)

genius emeritus, a

<u>Geronimo!</u> moment, a (para-
   troopers' battle cry)

Ghandi-meets-Martin-Luther-
   King-meets-Mother-Theresa

gifted

gilded moment, a

gilt-edged

gin! (card-game victory call)

glimmering of greatness, a

glimpse of paradise, a

glowingly great

g-o-a-a-l! (cry after score in
   soccer/European football)

goes the distance

goes the limit

goes whole hog

Golcondan (*ref.*, legendary
   Golconda mines in India:
   promising great wealth)

gold standard, the

gold-medal

golden goose, a

gold-plated

good to the yolk

goodness bottled and corked

gooz (good)

go-to guy/gal, the

gourmet reality

governs! (as in "it rules!")

grand

grand slam, a (*ref.*, baseball
   home run scoring four players:
   major payoff for an effort)

grandeur itself

graven on the cereal box

gravy

great from the git-go

great meets amazing

great served hot

great to the marrow

great with a tailwind

great with a vengeance

greater then superstrings (*ref.*,
   basic element in unified theory
   of the universe)

Greatness 301

greatness affirmed, avouched,
   and avowed

greatness bespangled

greatness bulked and pumped

greatness deciphered

greatness decoded

greatness emblazoned

greatness full-blown

greatness in a lesser guise

greatness in alto-relievo (high
   relief)

greatness in high relief

greatness in majuscules (large letters)
greatness laminated
greatness on Pegasus (mythical winged horse)
greatness spraddled, splayed, and spangled
greatness stockpiled
greatness unearthed
greatness unfurled
greatness with gusto
greatness writ large
Greatsville
green stuff
green-jacket (worn by golf Master's champions)
grudgingly perfect
guilty of greatness
hail-all-hail magnificent
hallelujah great
hallmark/hallmark, a
hall-of-fame
halo-wearing
hardly evanescent
hardly insignificant
hardly mediocre
hardly trifling
hardy
has greatness to burn
haute!

haymaker, a (full-force blow)
headliner, a
headline-worthy
heads-up (alert, competent)
heaven on a stick
heaven's gift
heaven-sent
heinously great
heir to all that is good, the
high roller, a (dice)
high signal-to-noise ratio (far more worthy content or character than unworthy)
high-definition body, a
high-domed (smart)
high-fiveable
high-five-worthy
high-performance
high-stakes
high-test (high-performance)
high-wire performance, a
historic
hog heaven
hole in one, a (golf)
honey pot, the
honeymoon!
honorable
honors humanity
hot dice
hot goods

hotcakes

hot-ticket

Hudson River landing, a (*ref.*, heroic 2009 landing of stalled passenger jet on river)

humbling

humiliatingly great

hundred-percenter, a

hyperkosher

iconic

ideal

illustrious

imbued with glory

immemorial

immortal

immutably brilliant (unchangingly)

impeccable

imperative experience, an

imperial

imposing

in a nutshell, perfect

in a word, extraordinary

in the flush of greatness

in the mojo zone

in the money

inclines toward perfection

incomparable

indispensible

inestimable (beyond estimating)

information, the

ingeniously inventive

ingot of greatness, an

innately great (born great)

inscribed in the register of great

insightful

inspired

instantaneously classic

insuperable (impossible to excel)

intensely good

it's all jake (all correct, satisfactory)

jack! (money)

jackpot

jarringly good

Jedi master, a (*ref.*, *Star Wars* knights: a highly skilled person)

jewel in the imperial crown, a

jubilantly brilliant

just run-of-the-mill perfect

just run-of-the-mill phenomenal

karma's darling (fate, destiny; reward for good life)

kayo, a

keen

keeper, a

kempt to the pleats and creases (neat)

kernel of perfection, the

keystone, the
killing
kills!
kindling flame, the
king's choice, a
kipper's knickers, the (*SCOT*)
kissed by kismet (fortune)
knightly
knockout/knockout, a
KO, a (kayo; boxing knockout)
kudos-worthy
landmark/landmark, a (highly
    significant)
large-minded
lastingly great
laudable
laurel-wearing
laurel-worthy
leather-bound, tooled, and gilded
leg up on perfect, a
legend (*IR*)
legendary
let it be engraved in gold
letter-perfect
level (*CAN*)
levitates! (as in "it rules!")
life force, a
lifelong keeper, a
linchpin, a (key factor in some-
    thing's success)

litterateur, a (scholar or creator
    of literature)
living large (living the flush
    lifestyle)
loaded for bear
loaves and fishes
locked and loaded
lodestar, a (guiding star)
lofty
long-established
long-standing
ludicrously superior
luminary, a (one shining with
    fame, achievement)
luminous
luxe-plus (luxury)
luxuriant specimen, a
luxury goods
maestro, a
magic
magical
magic-circle (elite)
magisterial
magnanimous (noble or lofty of
    mind, spirit)
Mahabharatumly epic (*ref.*, epic
    poem of India)
mahatma, a (person revered for
    wisdom)
majestic

major league

mandarin (high-ranking)

manically great

manifestly robust

manna (good thing coming unexpectedly)

March Madness (annual upbeat basketball frenzy)

mark of supremacy, the

marked for greatness

marquee name, a

marquee player, a

mashup of talents, a

masterstroke, a

masterful

masterly

mastermind, a

masterpiece, a

matchless

Mausoleum-of-King-Mausolas-at-Halicarnassus magnificent (*ref.*, Seven Ancient Wonders)

maven, a

maximum brilliant

Medal-of-Honor great

Mega Millions ticket, the (lottery)

meister, a (master)

Mensa material (high-IQ society)

mensch, a (reliable, upstanding person)

meritorious

meta- (*prefix:* about, beyond, after, within, superior)

metameta (beyond beyond)

milestone, a

milk and honey

milks a good cow (—Blake Nicholls via Bill Casselman: *CAN*, is in the money)

milk train, the

mind like a diamond saw

mind like a jeweler's saw

mind like a machete

mind like a scythe

miracle of the millennium, the

miraculous alchemy, a (transformation into something prized)

mission accomplished!

model

modern wonder of the world, a

momentous

money (someone attractive, successful, wonderful)

money tree, a

monsta!

monster-dividend, a

moored in excellence

most brammer (*Par.*, *UK*, excellent, outstanding)

mother lode, a
Mozartian
mugs! (as in "it rules!")
multiple of great, a
museum-quality
mythical
naked perfection
national resource, a
national treasure, a
natural, a
nature's gift
ne plus ultra, the (*L*.: highest
    point, ultimate degree)
nectar
never-to-be-forgotten
nimble
no Mickey Mouse
no slouch
nobby (chic, stylish)
no-hitter, a (perfect baseball
    pitching performance)
no-strings-attached perfection
not chopped herring
not exactly middling
not exactly nothing
not off the mark
not penny ante (not small stakes)
not shoddy
not unlearned
notable

notched up
note-on
nothing but net (clean basketball
    shot)
nothing less than the lifeblood
nub of the matter, the
'nuff-said brilliant
nulli secundus (*L*., second to
    none)
numba one
numero uno
odds-on best, the
odds-on favorite, the
of imposing grandeur
off the chart and the easel
offshoot of exquisite, an
oh, daddums!
oh, momma!
oh, mumsy!
oh, pappy!
Olympian
Olympic gold
on a tear
on the flag (accurate golf shot)
oofy (having money)
oozing with talent
optimal
optimum
ordains! (as in "it rules!")
Oscar-worthy

outlandishly great

outperforming

outrageously good

out-the-blowhole spectacular

ovational

ownage! (*ref.*, computer gaming: owns the competition, as in "rules!")

pace-setting

packed in mohair

paean-worthy (song of joyous praise)

Palatinate of Perfect, the

palmary (praiseworthy)

palmy (flourishing, prosperous)

pan-supreme (all-supreme)

pantingly great

paradigm, a (exemplary model)

paradigmatic (serving as a model)

paradise pie

paragon of dignity, a (model of)

paragon, a (model)

paramount (supreme in rank)

parliament of owls, mind like a

pathway to perfection, a

pay dirt!

pay twenty-one! (blackjack-winning call)

payday

payload, the

payoff, the

peak of perfect, the

pedigreed

peerless

pelf! (money)

people's laureate, the

percolating (doing fine)

perfection boxed, bottled, and canned

perfection inscribed on parchment

perfection made to order

perfection on the nose

perfection pickled and preserved

perfection signed, sealed, and delivered

perfection spelled out

perfection with a Ph.D.

perfection wrapped and bundled

perfection writ large

perfection's doppelgänger (double)

phat 2 death (*rap*: fine, excellent)

phenom, a (fee-nom—a phenomenon)

phenomenal

Picasso!

pillar of greatness, a

pillar-to-post perfect

pinnacle, the

pinnacular (peaklike)

pioneering

pitch-perfect

pith and core of excellence, the

pithy

pivotal

pièce de résistance, the (*Fr.*: showpiece)

platinum

platinum standard, the

platinum-level (as with credit card or memberships)

playbook-perfect

player, a

Pleasure-Dome dazzling

pleo- (*prefix*: more)

pleoperfect

plumbed and squared

plunders! (as in "it rules!")

poetry! (having the grace of poetry)

point man, a (lead soldier, lookout, in a patrol)

polyphiloprogenitive (prolifically talented, inventive)

posh!

postcard-perfect

pot o' simoleons, a (*ref.*, *The Sims* game series: dollars)

powerfully expressive

preeminent

preposterously great

preposterously perfect

presto miracle, a (sudden and quick)

prevailing

prime

prime mover, the

prime shaker, the

primed!

primed, charged, and cocked

prime-time-worthy

primo

princely

Principality of Perfect, the

prized

prodigy, a

prone to success

propagator of good, a

prosperous

providential

pukka (authentic, genuine)

punches out great's headlights

pundit, a

pure clover

pyrotechnically brilliant

quality goods, the

Queen Elizabeth at full steam, a

queenly

Quicksilver Eddie Aikau! (top surfing prize)

rad redux (old term "rad" brought back)

raging good

rarefied (distinct from the ordinary, purged of coarseness)

raveworthy

raving good

real gazookus, the (genuine article)

real merchandise, the

red-carpet

red-letter (joyful or festive, as in red-letter day)

red-letter event, a

reeducation, a

refined

refulgent (radiant)

regal!

regal bearing, a

reigns! (as in "it rules!")

remarkable

Rembrandt!

repository of excellence, a

resounding

resplendent (splendid, dazzling)

resplendently brilliant

result! (UK, exclamation at success)

reverberant

reverberatingly great

revered

rich

rich harvest, a

riddled with genius

rigged fore and aft

right stuff, the

rightful

right-thinking

rinsin'! (Par., UK, cheer to disc jockey "rinsing" or mixing tunes; well done!)

risibly superior (laughably)

roaringly intelligent

Rolls-Royce

romp, a

Rose Bowl!

round-tripper, a (baseball home run)

rout, a

royal

royal flush, a (high poker hand)

rules the roost

runaway best, the

running at full sail

running before the wind (sailing)

runs the rack (ref., all pool balls sunk)

sack o' C-notes, a (hundred-dollar bills)

saddled on Pegasus (mythical winged horse)

saddled on Seabiscuit (famed racehorse)

saddled on Secretariat (famed racehorse)

sage

sagacious (wise)

salute-worthy

sans pareil (*Fr.*: unequalled)

sapient (wise, learned)

savant, a (wise person)

savor of excellence, a

screamer-headline worthy

screaming great

seal of greatness, the

seamless

seamlessly fine

seamlessly woven

seize-the-day special

selecta! (*UK*, shout of approval, parodied by comic Ali G)

sensational, short-and-sweet

seriously good

set-off-the-fireworks great

seventy-two-point worthy (large type size)

shepherd of humankind, a

shiznit, the (*rap, semi-vulgar*: the most excellent, the best)

shizzy (*rap*, good quality)

shoots the works

shoulder-to-shoulder with perfection

shower-of-sparks brilliant

showstopper, a

showstopping

showpiece, the

shredding

shreds! (as in "it rules!")

shrewd in spades

signal

signally good

silk-stocking (upper-class, aristocratic)

silky

silver on silk

silver-circle (elite, as in high-end law firms)

sinewed

skinny, the

skizziest, the

skookum (*CAN*, good, brave, strong, cool)

skybox

slam-dunk, a (assertive basketball shot)

slap shot, a (hockey)

slaying

slippy (*UK*, nimble)

smack-in-the-glove perfect (*ref.*, solid throw to baseball glove)

smacks of greatness

smacks of perfection

smoked!

so great it's almost wrong

socko-boffo

some bit of stuff

something to tweet about

sovereign

sower of goodness, a

spectacular in 3-D

spikeable (*ref.*, football "spiked" to ground after touchdown: achievement completed)

spit-and-polish perfection

splendidious

splits the fairway (excellent golf shot from tee)

spot-on

spouter, a (oil-drilling jargon for good well)

Sprint Cup, the (NASCAR trophy)

spumescently brilliant (foamingly)

stand-up (solid, dependable, loyal)

Stanley Cup! (top hockey prize)

stark-staring marvelous

stately

state-of-the-art

stay in Utopia, a

steadfastly great

Steinway-quality

stellar

steppin' out like Native Dancer (famed racehorse)

sterling

stoater, a (*SCOT*, an excellent something or female someone)

stoating (*SCOT*, excellent)

stone-ground good

storied

storming (*UK*)

storybook

Stradivarian (rare and precious, like the famed violins)

straight-ahead

studly

study in excellence, a

stunner, a

stupendous, stamped and delivered

sui generis (*L*.: unique of its kind)

sultan's choice, a

sum and substance, the

summital

Super Bowl!
superachieving
superbissimo (*UK*, mock-Italian
　intensification of superb)
supersweet
supreme artistry
supremo
surface-to-air spectacular
surpassing
swashbuckling
swathed in goodness
sweeps the board (wins all the
　prizes, votes, etc.)
sweet!
sweet-melon mellow
take it to the bank
takes a victory lap
takes the cake and eats it, too
Tarzanesque
TD! (football touchdown)
team terrific
tectonically great (with force of
　plates of earth's crust)
tempered torso, a (hardened)
ten-curtain-call performance, a
ten-o'clock highlight, a (*ref.*, TV
　news)
Terra Terrific
textbook
that's a wrap! (completion of

a successful shoot in film or
　video)
thoroughbred
three-hundred game, a (perfect
　bowling score)
three-point landing, a
thrummingly great
thundering
thwackingly great
tight!
time-honored
timeless
title holder, the
TKO, a (boxing, technical
　knockout)
to bleed for
to cark for (die)
to croak for
to cut to the chase, extraordinary
to cut to the chase, unparalleled
to die in the ditch for
to drown for
to flatline for
to give up the ghost for
to pass over Jordan for
to perish for
to shed one's skin for
to starve for
toda madre, a (*Sp.*: full-bore,
　excellent)

top billing
top of the class
top-banana
top-drawer (*UK*)
topflight
topping (excellent, *UK*)
top-shelf
touché! (scored point in fencing)
touchstone, a (standard for judging)
trailblazing
tramples! (as in "it rules!")
transformative
trifecta, the (lucrative bet picking three winners in correct order)
trig (neat, smart, trim; in good condition)
trill (*rap*: true and real)
triple threat, a (multi-skilled, as in athletics)
triple-axel perfect (ice skating)
triple-crown (winner in three major categories/events of baseball/racing)
triplicity of excellence, a
triumph of overreach, a
triumphant
trophy-winning
trove, a
trump card, the (something valu-able held for key advantage)
trumps all
tweetworthy
twin killing, a (victory in a baseball doubleheader)
ultimate best, an
ultima Thule, the (*L.*: the ultimate reachable point or ideal)
ultimate, the
unabashedly best
unadorned perfection
unalloyed goods, the
unbad
uncontested
undisputed champ, the
undreamed-of
undyingly great
unequivocally fine (absolutely, unambiguously)
unforgettable
uniformly good
unimpeachably great
unlame
unpresumingly brilliant
unreservedly brilliant
unshatterable integrity, of
untarnished
unthinkable feat, an
up there
up to its ears in excellence

upper-case great
upper-crust
upright and reputable
uptown
vanguard
varsity!
velvet
velvet-rope territory, in
venerable
venerated
vertiginously good (—Dwight
  Garner: dizzyingly)
VG ("very good")
victory-arch worthy
victory-lapper, a
virtuoso
visionary
walking force field, a
walking power grid, a
walk-off homer, a (game-ending
  home run in baseball)
walks on bubbly
walks on Evian (bottled water
  brand)
walks on Perrier (bottled water
  brand)
walks on vodka
wanting in nothing
warhead for good, a
well bred

well knit
wellspring of excellence, a
what great aspires to
whiff of perfection, a
white lightning
white-smoke happening, a (ref.,
  announcement of new pope)
whole package, the
whole taxonomy of virtues, a
why and wherefore, the
wields the scepter! (as in "it
  rules!")
wildfire
Wimbledon!
wings-out and wafting
wins in a walk
with éclat (dazzling brilliance;
  showy effect; conspicuous
  success)
without mincing words, "super-
  califragilisticexpialidocious"
  (from film Mary Poppins)
wizzy (UK)
wonder-working
wondrous without end
works the strings
world beater, a
world class
World Cup!
World Series!

worthy of the royal diadem
  (crown)
wowser, a
wreathed in greatness
written in the Book of Life
wunderkind, a
X-Men-like
you bagged it!
you blazed!
you butchered!
you caught a high flyer (high-
  paying volatile stock)
you clinched it!

you couldn't handle how great
you detonated!
you don't even want to know
  how great
you drubbed!
you flushed it!
you iced it!
you oxidized!
you ran the table!
you rolled a natural! (a winning
  7 or 11 in dice)
you scalped!
you throttled!

VINTAGE GOLD

bears the bell
bourbonified
copacetic
copper-bottomed
corker, the
crackerjack
dandy
darb, the
dilly, a
ducky
doozie, a
george
humdinger, a
Jim Dandy
lollapalooza
lulu, a
nifty
nuts, the
pipperoo, a
right as a trivet
ripsniptious
topnotch
ultra-ultra

OXYMORONICALLY CLEVER: INTENSIFYING WITH CONTRARY MODIFIERS

When deftly employed, an oxymoron or paradoxical modifier (for example, something bad modifying something good) can mean "to such a degree that it turns values upside down." Following are a group of forceful adjectives that can be turned into adverbs (add "-ly") and paired with positive traits such as "great," "gorgeous," "talented," "clever," "tasty," etc., for ironic effect. For example: *scathing* + *ly* paired with *talented* = *scathingly talented*. A good thing.

aberrant

atrocious

baneful

barbarous

belligerent

bestial

biting

catastrophic

corrosive

cutting

damnable

demolishing

demoniac

deviant

diabolic

distressing

eviscerating

felonious

fierce

flagrant

flaunting

freakish

glaring

grating

(CONTINUED)

{CONTINUED}

insufferable

malefic

perverse

sanguineous (involving
  bloodshed)

savage

scathing

scorching

scurrilous

shameful

sharkish

sinful

sinister

snaky (snakily)

sneering

subversive

swaggering

tart

transgressive

unlawful

unmerciful

unsparing

villainous

virulent

withering

(See similar locutions under
  "Wicked Cool")

SUBLIME

* **Exalted**
* **Divine**
* **Holy**
* **Of Sacred Perfection**

BEYOND THE KEN OF CRITTERS

If animals were learning English, would they need loftier terms than *yummy* or *comfy* to acclaim their favorite things? To a critter's mind, a good chew and a funky cushion might be as good as things get.

To our minds, however, certain exalted things cannot be lumped with the golf shots, hairdos, and chewy mouthfuls we call *great* or *terrific*. Unlike our animal companions, we have a notion of entities and concepts that transcend such terms. We place these higher things in a category sometimes called "the sublime" or "the sacred," and we acclaim them with elevated language.

As our list shows, much of the sublime has to do with religion—reverence for the divine and holy—and with the often-related qualities of perfection and purity. Acclaim such as *almighty* or *all-embracing* is usually reserved for one's deities, but *heavenly* and its synonyms (*celestial*, *empyreal*, *supernal*) might be applied to things that merely approach the qualities (and height) of the Holy Kingdom.

The perfection addressed under our "Great" category is the worldly kind—the "perfect rice every time," the "perfect-game" pitching performance in baseball. But under "Sublime," we are in the realm of perfection *beyond judgment*, of the *omega point* and *pure pneuma* (see definitions).

While sublimity is serious business, its acclaim is not always without personality. A playful phrase like *whelp of the gods* still lofts one above mortals. What does taint the sublimity of a term is its application to anyone and anything, as in trivializations of *Tao* (ultimate reality) from "the Tao of Poker" to "the Tao of Tattoos." Or think of all the cheesy products we call *pure*. Before you know it someone will be calling me *seraphic* at the least beating of my wings.

TERMS

absolved of wrong
afflated (having a divine inspiration from within)
afflatus, an (breath of divine inspiration from within)
algorithm of perfection, an
all-embracing
appearing to humankind)
anointed
apotheosis, an (deification, exalted example, most glorious level)
archangelic
arrived at Kingdom Come

> "Walking [on a tightwire] was a divine delight. Everything was rewritten when he was up in the air. New things were possible with the human form. It went *beyond equilibrium*. He felt for a moment uncreated. Another kind of awake."
>
> —Colum McCann, *Let the Great World Spin*, 2009

all-knowing
all-pervading
all-powerful
almighty
angel-hatched
angelical
angelophanic (*ref.*, angels
ascendant
astral (elevated like the stars, exalted)
astrogation to divine light, an (*ref.*, spacecraft navigation)
at the threshold of divine
atman, of the (universal soul or

spirit, Hinduism)

aubade to the dawn of perfection, an (song or poem greeting the dawn or morning)

awakening, an

beatific (of heavenly bliss)

beatified (made sacredly blissful; declared holy)

beau ideal, the (perfect or idealized type or model)

benediction, a

beyond appellation

beyond appraisal

beyond equilibrium

beyond judgment

beyond utterance

blessed

Brahmin (high-priestly)

buddhi-driven (*ref.*, intuitive, truth-discerning intellect, Hinduism)

called (summoned, as if by divinity)

Camelot, a

canonical

celestial

cheek by jowl with perfection

chosen, the

Christlike

churchlike sanctity, a

City Celestial, of (heavenly)

cloud-piercingly ascendant

communion with grace, a

communion with perfection, a

consecrated (set apart as sacred)

cut above perfection, a

cynosure of devotion, a (attracting devotion)

cynosure of piety, a (attracting piety)

darshan moment, a (seeing a holy personage or deity, Hinduism)

deathless

defies denomination

demigod, a

devotion-worthy

divine breath, a

divine grandeur

divinity incarnate

Eden refreshed

elevated

elysian (yielding paradisal bliss)

Elysium, an/ Elysian Fields, the (Ancient Greek heaven; blissful place or state)

emblem of perfection, an

empyreal (celestial, of the empyrean or heavens)

enlightened one, the

ennobled

enshrined
enskyed (placed in the heavens)
enthroned
epiphanic (yielding epiphany,
    revelation)
eternal
etheric plane, the (neo-
    Theosophical/Rosicrucian
    higher plane of existence)
eudaemonic (conducive to
    reason-based happiness)

God's dream manifest
God's opus
god-begotten
"God-breathed" (—2 Timothy
    3:16)
godlike
gone home to the Promised Land
gone home to Zion
graced
grovel-at-the-feet-of divine
hallowed

"How it cleaves the *empyrean* and makes the *welkin* ring
as it glitters in the sunshine of high noon...."

—Montgomery Schuyler,
of the Woolworth Building, Manhattan, 1913

everlasting light, the
evokes the gods
exalted
fall-back-in-awe supreme
fall-prostrate-before sublime
fruit of infinite prayers, the
full of grace
genuflection-worthy
glorious
God's music

heaven here and now
heaven-born
heavenly
heaven-minted
holiness embodied
Holy Grail, the (lofty goal; spiri-
    tual union with the divine)
hymned and canticled (praised
    by song)
immortal

in peak experience (state of transcendent ecstatic, religious, epiphanic experience)

in the bosom of Abraham (received in heaven)

incommensurably great (nothing can be measured against it)

incomprehensibly divine

inconceivable, the

ineffable (beyond expression)

ineluctable power, the (inescapable)

inenarrable (beyond narration)

inerrant (free of error; infallible)

inestimable (too great to estimate)

infallible

Infinite One, the

innominate (unnamable)

inspired

intimation of sublimity, an

kin to perfection

land of milk and honey, a

lapidary perfection (precisely engraved)

let-it-be-adulated-extolled-and-adored

let-it-be-glorified

let-it-be-hallelujahed

let-it-be-hosanna'd

let-it-be-praised

let-it-be-sung-in-hymns-and-paeans

let-it-be-worshipped

"Lifter up of mine head" (—St. Augustine, *The City of God*)

Light, The

lofty

maha (*Hin.*: great, as in maharishi, "great seer")

Messianic

mosquelike

music of the celestial spheres (perfect harmony)

naked perfection, of

New Jerusalem, the (heaven to come)

nirvanic (*ref.*, Buddhist/Hindu nirvana or elevated state)

numinous (spiritually elevated; filled with sense of supernatural presence)

oblation, an (gift offering to the gods)

of papal majesty

of the City of God (forgoes earthly pleasures and glory, Christianity)

Olympian

Olympus-bound

omega point, the (theologian's term for ultimate evolution of human consciousness)

omnipotent

omniscient (all-knowing)

on an astral plane

Osirian (like Egyptian god of the dead Osiris, whose annual resurrection symbolizes renewal)

pantheonic (suitable as a temple for gods)

paradisal

paradise here and now

Perfect Master, the (highest rank in certain spiritual systems)

perfection crystallized

perfection embodied

perfection imprinted

pierces the empyrean (the highest heaven)

pierces/touches heaven's vault

portentous (marvelous, wonderful; also, foreboding ill)

portrait of perfection, a

prelapsarian (of the time or state before the fall of Adam and Eve)

pretersensual (beyond what can be sensed)

priestly

prime mover, the

prostrate oneself before, to

providential

pure anima (soul)

pure pneuma (soul, Stoicism)

purified

purusha, of the (eternal soul or self, Hinduism)

pyx, a (container to hold the Eucharist; container of precious things)

quail-before-it perfection

quaver-at-its-name sublime

quintessential (representing the most perfect embodiment)

Rapture, the (ascension of Christian souls gathered to meet Christ)

rapturous

redemption of humankind, a

revelation, a

revelational

rings the welkin (vault of heaven)

risen to Elysium

saintly

samadhi (Hindu/Buddhist highest state of consciousness, oneness with universe) sanctified

satori (Zen Buddhist sudden awakening to reality)

seraph, a (angel of highest order)

seraphic

"Sire of an immortal strain" (—Percy Bysshe Shelley, "Adonaïs")

snippet of the sublime, a

sojourn through paradise, a

supersensible (beyond sense perception)

supersensual (beyond range of the senses; spiritual)

supreme

tabernacle, of the (container/ sanctuary of sacred items)

Tao, the (ultimate reality)

templelike

theophanous-like (like a deity

"America was charmed by Obama's *supernal* speeches...."

—Charles M. Blow,
New York Times, June 19, 2010

---

sovereign

splendorous

state of sublimity, a

stone's throw from sublime, a

sublime

suffused with grace

summa cum laude (earning highest praise)

summons to worship, a

supernal (exalted to heaven; celestial, greater than earthly)

appearing before one)

theophany, a (appearance of a deity before a person)

"thrice and four times blessed" (—Virgil, *The Aeneid*)

"throned in highest bliss" (—John Milton, *Paradise Lost*)

totemic (emblematic or symbolic of something venerated)

transcendent

transfiguration, a (transforming

of appearance revealing
  exalted quality)
transfinite (surpassing the finite)
triplicity of perfection, a
undefiled
unerring
unfathomable
unquestionable, the
unspeakably majestic
unspotted

unutterably glorious
unutterably holy
Valhalla-bound
vision mirabilis, a (miraculous)
visitation, a
Way, The
whelp of the gods, a (child, pup)

"[T]he band upon the stage like a *visitation* from a world of rhythm."

—Junot Díaz,
The Brief Wondrous Life of Oscar Wao, 2007

PHYSICALLY AFFECTING

* **Having Impact on One's Body or Its Parts**
* **Metaphorically Affecting One's Body or Its Parts**

PRAISE BY HURTS AND TICKLES

Think about the most intense pleasure you've had in one body part (easy, now!) and the worst pain you've had in another. Then consider novelist José Saramago's observation that "in order to invent heaven and hell, ... [one] would need to know nothing except the human body."

Knowing our bodies—and how things affect them—certainly helps us describe the here and now, if not necessarily the hereafter. Bodies speak a universal language. We can characterize something by its perceived physical impact (e.g., *knee-weakening*) or by an exaggerated symbolic impact (*tongue-twisting*). When we want to be persuasive, such description offers the possibility of empathetic response—of being felt. Make them feel it in the body part, and they pay attention. Franz Kafka famously said that a book should "wake us up with a blow on the head."

Like all figures of speech, however, body-based metaphors get worn out; they become white noise. Driving such figures home usually calls for verbal inventiveness. The term *side-splitting* has been around some 150 years, and, though occasionally serviceable, it no longer agitates my flanks and turns them toward the acclaimed source. I would be more persuaded by such novel acclaim as "gets up your nose!" (based on Salman Rushdie's image of comedy: that it "gets up people's noses"). This I can feel all the way to my sinuses, and I take heed.

It may seem odd that physical pain or distress can play a role in praise and acclamation. Do we really want our eyes to pop free at an eye-popping spectacle? Our blood to run cold at a horror film? What sells such things is not true danger, but the edginess of the thought—that while something claims the power to pop the eyes, we will experience only the keen emotional feeling and not the dangling orbs.

People do find certain modestly punishing experiences

to be praiseworthy: a sportscar's *body-slamming* acceleration; a *butterflies-inducing* love affair; a *stomach-churning* roller coaster. But most pain associated with praise is of the imaginary sort, the nerve shatterings and electrifications threatened by various diversions, but not to be inflicted.

In practice, much of this acclaim turns up in critical writing, in reviews, where brief, punchy expression fits the format and gives rise to compound, hyphenated modifiers (Germanisms): *gut-wrenching*; *set-your-hair-on-fire shocking*. Agile critics and other writers invent entirely new modifiers—new body parts receiving new actions—or freshen up a worn modifier by changing one of its elements to something both novel and imaginable. For example, the clenching action has lost some of its bite in such clichés as *jaw-clenching suspense*, but when writer T. C. Boyle plugs in a new body part (see quote in the list that follows), the force returns.

Writers for the BBC spy series *MI-5* found still another anatomical part to be clenched for effect: An agent speaks of "chest-tearing, *bum-clenching* boredom." Bum (butt)-clenching might not have the ring of acclaim for everything, but for boredom it's a clangorous compliment.

TERMS

abrading
acorn-pickling (slang for
   testicles)
battering
beard-lifting

bosom-heating
breath-abating (shortening or
   stopping breath)
breath-quickening
brow-raising

"[Would] put the heart crossways"
          —Tana French, *Faithful Place*, 2010

bed-of-thorns awakening
blanching (whitening, making
   pale)
blistering
blood-fizzing
blood-spiking
blood-stewing
body-slamming
bone-melting
bone-shaking
bong for the brain, a
booty-warming

bum-clenching (—*MI-5* television series, "Spooks," 2002)
butt-puckering
cheek-burning
chest-caving
chest-tearing
chest-tightening
clammy-making
cold-cocking (knocking out)
concussive
contusive (bruising)
deracinating (uprooting)

dizzying

dopamine storm, a (pleasure-related brain chemical)

electrifying

electrocuting

endocrine-stirring

endorphin blizzard, an (feel-good brain secretion)

endorphining

eye-bulging

eye-misting

face-caving

fat-jiggling

febrifacient (fever-making)

feel-goodant, a

flesh-rippling

flooring

fracturing

gets your belly in a polka (—Bonnie Grove)

gets your girls disco-dancing (girls = slang for breasts)

gland-milking

gonad-shrinking

gut-tingling

hair-scorching

hair-spronging

head-banging

head-swerving

head-toppling

heart-blanching

heart-braising

heart-chafing

heart-chafingly poignant

heart-dicing

heart-fizzing

heart-fluttering

heart-juddering (vibrating)

heart-nudging

heart-nuking

heart-piercing

heart-quickening

heart-rasping

heart-stewing

heart-strafing

heart-throttling

"If that advice makes your insides do the happy dance, may I suggest a writing book that will really *get your belly in a polka*."

—Bonnie Grove, fictionmatters.blogspot.com, Oct. 14, 2009

heart-twiddling
heart-twitching
heart-walloping
heart-wiltingly tender
horripilatingly scary (causes
  one's hair to bristle)
incapacitating

like an intercontinental ballistic
  missile to your gut
makes your duff get going
makes your heart warble
makes your insides do a happy
  dance (—Bonnie Grove)
marrow-churning

"I could a tale unfold whose lightest word
Would harrow up thy soul; freeze thy young blood;
Make thy two eyes, like stars, start from their spheres;
Thy knotted and combined locks to part,
And each particular hair to stand on end,
Like quills upon a fretful porcupine: ..."
—William Shakespeare, *Hamlet*, 1.5

---

inebriating
intoxicating
invigorating
jaw-slacking
joint-freezing
knee-jellying
knee-wobbling
leg-shaking
like a submarine-killer rocket to
  your cortex
like an air-to-air missile through
  your head

marrow-freezingly scary
mauling
mouth-dessicating (drying up)
nerve-frazzling
nerve-nuking
nerve-quivering
nerve-yanking
numbing
palm-moistening
palpitation-making
palpitator, a
po-po-warming

> "If I feel physically as if the top of my head were taken off, I know that is poetry."
>
> —Emily Dickinson,
> quoted by Thomas Wentworth Higginson

pulls your pants off
pulse-raising
puts your brain in high-def
puts your cells in double mitosis
puts your heart in silly season
puts your hormones in overdrive
queeving (energy-draining)
quiver-giving
salt-on-the-wound stimulating
sawed-off-shotgun staggering
scrotum-scrunchingly scary
shirt/blouse-drenching
shock-therapeutic
shpilkes-making (*Yi.*: pins and needles)
skin-tightening shocker, a
skull-denting
stabbing
stack-blowing
staggering
stammer-and-stutter-making
Stendahl-syndrome trigger, a (psychosomatic dizziness, palpitation, fainting, confusion caused by exposure to a concentration of beautiful art. Also "Florence syndrome.")
stunning
stutter-causing
three-stage pulse-booster, a
throat-tightening
tongue-dryingly awesome
tongue-thickening
tread-on-coals stimulating
tremor-making
unbalancing

> "I became aware of the intense, gland-clenching aroma of vanilla chai."
> —T. C. Boyle, "The Lie," *New Yorker*, April 14, 2008

will bounce your boys (boys =
    slang for testicles)
will carbonate your hormones
will hammer your chimes
will jiggle your chimes

will rattle your stones
will reset your equilibrium
will skyrocket your skivvies
will spike your endocrines

TWENTY SERVICEABLE
OLD STANDBYS

bloodcurdling
bloodstirring
bone-chilling
butt-kicking
eye-catching
eye-opening
eye-popping
gets under the skin
gut-wrenching
hair-raising
heartaching
heartbreaking
heartstirring
jaw-dropping
kick-ass
knee-weakening
makes the blood run cold
nerve-tingling
pulse-quickening
rib-tickling

MENTALLY, EMOTIONALLY, OR SPIRITUALLY AFFECTING

* **Moving**
* **Exciting**
* **Amazing**
* **Wondrous**
* **Attention-Getting**
  (See also under: "Joy-Giving")

POWERING THE EMOTIONAL MISSILE

One hears much lately, especially in military strategy, of "winning the hearts and minds" of people. Such victory might hinge on reconstruction and the greasing of palms, but one of the oldest methods of winning the love—of getting people to embrace something—is to extol that thing's impact on the inner life.

The technique plays out in propaganda (*freeing, transformative, energizing*); in advertising blurbs (*amazing, hypnotic, thrilling*); and promotion of artistic and intellectual endeavors (*edifying, illuminating, spellbinding*). From the beginnings of literature, writers have glorified people and events by hyping their mental, emotional, or spiritual impact. Just how admirable is the hero of the epic *Beowulf*? He has saved chieftain Hrothgar's people, yes; but Hrothgar's emotional response to his savior is even more persuasive:

> his breast's wild billows he [Hrothgar] banned in vain;
> safe in his soul a secret longing,
> locked in his mind, for that loved man
> burned in his blood." ... (*Beowulf*, XXVI)

While such acclaim suits a 1,400-year-old world of mead halls, I'd be proud today to be dubbed a breast-billower.

In today's watering holes, acclaim referencing the inner life usually peaks at *amazing* or *mind-blowing*, but journalism and literature yield powerful models for the intrepid seeker. Open a volume of ultimate acclaimer Walt Whitman and see how certain things arouse "the mystic deliria—the madness amorous—the utter abandonment." Meanwhile, I offer what I hope are idea-triggering suggestions in the following list and in the related categories "Joy-Giving" and "Challenging Belief."

Speaking of categories, I should note that within

several I incorporate the words *heart* and *brain* into suggested terms. *Brain* is usually meant metaphorically, not in the sense of a shivering gray physical mass; but *heart* is sometimes considered a physical organ to be figuratively jostled (*heart-juddering*) and sometimes itself a metaphor for feelings (*heart-plundering*). I may be slipping semantic and categorical boundaries; but if a term wins your heart and mind, consider me *transported*.

TERMS

absorbing
affecting
Amazement City
amazement, an
amazing unleashed
amen-astonishing
animating
arresting
astrogation through inner space, an (*ref.*, spacecraft navigation)
"axe for the frozen sea inside us, the" (—Franz Kafka, what a book must be, 1904)
bewitching
beyond boggling
both-barrels mind-blasting
brain-bifurcating
brain-bludgeoning
brain-crashing
brain-draining
brain-incinerating
brain-pulverizing
brains-into-putty astonishing
brain-stunning

brain-waffling
brass-knuckles stupefying
captivating
commoving (agitating, exciting)
consuming
daft-making
disembodying
dislocatingly amazing
double-take amazing
double-whammying
drainingly emotional
dumbstriking
dumfounding
edifying
emotional eggbeater, an
emotional liftoff, an
emotional splashdown, an
energizing
engaging
enlightening
enlightenment, an
enrapturing
enravishing
enthralling

entrancing
fascinating
flagellation of the senses, a
frisson, a (shudder of emotion)
gear-grindingly jolting
haunting
head-crumbling
heart-flurrying (bewildering)
heart-plundering

incantatory (enchanting, as by
    incantation)
incarnation of amazing, the
inspiriting
jaw-breakingly amazing
jitters-making
keenly affecting
kick-starts the spirit
like a meteorite through the soul

"Likewise the youth ... beheld a charming object, whose
heart-plundering face the handmaid of divine handicraft
had adorned with the blushing taint of grace...."
    —Hassain Waiz Kashifí, *The Anwári Sohailí*, 7th Book

---

heart-rustling
heart-twiddling
hot sauce for the brain
hypnotic
illuminating
impactive

make-way-for-it amazing
Mausoleum-of-King-Mausolas-
    at-Halicarnassus amazing (*ref.*,
    one of Seven Ancient Wonders)
meshuga-making (*Yi.*: crazy)
mesmeric

"[Mick Jagger is a] writer of brilliant, soulful, soaring,
incantatory anthems, hymns to broken hearts ... broken
spirits ... and fragmentary hopes for redemption...."
    —Ron Rosenbaum, *New York Observer*, Dec. 9, 2001

mesmerizing

meteor shower in the mind, a

Mind-Boggle Boulevard

mind-bonking

mind-broadening

mind-clobbering

mind-cudgeling

mind-diddling

mind-dismantling

mind-flummoxing

mind-freaking

mind-gutting

mind-hemorrhaging

mind-jangling

mind-joggling

mind-marmalizing (turning to marmalade)

mind-mussing

mind-mutilating

mind-probing

mind-pummeling

mind-razing

mind-rocketing

mind-ruffling

mind-scorching

mind-scrambling

mind-snatching

mind-stewing

mind-tripping

neuron-blasting

noodle-frying

nut-cracking

nutso-making

nuzzles the heart

passion-raising

peal of epiphanic insight, a (an epiphany)

pepper for the brain

propelling

provocative

provoking

psychic reentry, a

punch-drunk dizzying

quickening

quiver-making

R & R for the soul

riveting

rousing

run-of-the-mill stupefying

scalp-tightening

sending (emotionally moving)

sense-stunning

sit-down-and-brace-yourself amazing

soul-bracing

soul-churning

soul-flensing (flaying, skinning)

soul-freshening

soul-jiggling

soul-kindling

soul-laundering
soul-nourishing
soul-scouring
soul-seizing
soul-shearing
soul-smiting
soul-sparking
soul-throttling
soul-tugging
speech-foozling (bungling)
spellbinding
spellful
spirit-bracing
spirit-buoying
spiritual feeding frenzy, a
spiritual propellant, a
spiritual purgation, a
spiritual *schvitz*, a (*Yi.*: sweat
    bath)
spiritual soft landing, a
spiritual tonic, a
spiritual whiplash, a
startling
stirring
stirs your pudding
stupefying
surface-to-air uplift, a
swivet-making
    (excited nervousness)
terra firma for the spirit

thought-foozling (bungling)
thrillifying
tochis-over-teakettle trauma-
    tizing (*Yi.*: *tochis* = posterior)
tongue-cleaved-to-the-roof-of-
    the-mouth astounding
touching
transforming
transporting
trauma-making
traumatic
traumatizing
traumatizingly good
tumult-making
ungluing
vivifying
wake-the-dead amazing
wake-up beanball, a
wacko-making
will put your brains in a blender
will supercharge your psyche
will synchronize your clock
wit-sharpening

BEAUTIFUL

* **Appealing to the Senses**
* **Handsome**
* **Seductive**
  (See also under: "Delicious" and "Joy-Giving")

UNTYING THE BEAUTY-BOUND TONGUE

The presence of exceptional beauty inspires us to sing its praises, to let the world know how moved we are by the artwork, the sunset, a face across the room, whatever has enchanted us. But not everyone can trill a rhapsody in the heat of enchantment. Beauty's tongue-tying power alone can reduce our song to a few old notes. Maybe *beautiful.* Or *gorgeous.*

Even if we could uncork an arpeggio of adjectives on the spot, we'd probably come off like a trained parrot, or at least sound rehearsed. Sometimes the most convincing impromptu language is nonverbal—goo-goo eyes, chest-clutching, staggering collapses.

But later—perhaps in a love note or travel story or critical review—we want that special beauty to be understood as special. We want to distinguish its effect from that of ordinary beauty. We want it seen through our discerning eyes. We want our personal spin on the telling.

All that work cannot be accomplished just with adjectives and metaphoric nouns, not even ambitious ones like *ensorcelling* (bewitching) or *an Eden*. Persuasive acclaim calls for the whole package of rhetoric, not just labels. But stimulating labels—the suggestions in our lists—help sell the package.

What stimulates people in the way of beauty? Perhaps an unforgettable sensory quality like luminosity (*effulgent*) or sweet sound (*mellifluous*). Association with divine art (*Michelangelian*) or with a precious substance (*aureate*) might start the buzz. Or it might be the commotion stirred in others (*head-turner*) or ourselves, where the response might range from sacred (*enshrinable*) to profane (*bootylicious*). Perfect beauty can make us angry: It's not fair unless it's ours! We praise it in curiously paradoxical terms alleging outrage or suffering: *actionably gorgeous, criminally handsome; dolorously, irksomely, stabbingly, murderously beautiful.*

Then, too, beauty stirs sexual eros, winning acclaim for qualities of arousal. Years ago when I ground out sexy pulp novels to make ends meet, I compiled lists of modifiers to, shall we say, "beautify" various erogenous parts. Many an orb did I acclaim as *rotund* and *rosy*, many a haunch *supple* and *pliant*. Our language was legally restricted, rather purple, and far less graphic than the sometimes imaginative if degrading "praise" of beauty one hears on the streets. Likewise, in the list following, I've offered some PG-rated nods to eros (*badonkadonked*, *stud muffin*) along with modern-family-friendly terms like *nubile*.

For acclaiming good looks and sexy attributes, the golden age of slang—at least in America—was probably about 1910 to 1950, spiced by two world wars. I've included some samples in this section's "Vintage Gold."

TERMS

abidingly handsome
abloom
actionably gorgeous
adductively alluring (drawing one deep inside)
against-the-law gorgeous
against-the-law handsome
alluring
almond-eyed
amaranthine (unfadingly beautiful)
aphrodisiacal (stimulating sexual desire)
Apollo, an
Apollonian
arabesquely beautiful (complex, florid)
argentine (silvery)
arm candy
armed-to-the-neck seductive
armor-piercing looks
arrantly beautiful (utterly, immoderately)
artisanal masterwork, an (craft)

attar of allure, an (perfume or essential oil)
audaciously beautiful
aureate (brilliant gold)
auroral splendor, an (dawn- or auroralike)
Ava Gardner 2.0 (*ref.*, improved software release or version)
backlogged in sensuality
bada-bing, bada-boom!
badonkadonked/badunkadunked (having sexy buttocks)
ballet of swans, graceful as a
balsam of Mecca, a
beast-calming beauty
beauty aglow
beauty blazened
beauty bottled
beauty brandished and thrust home
beauty buffed and burnished
beauty crystallized
beauty embodied
beauty in full blossom

beauty in its prime
beauty on a binge
beauty to embosom (cherish, hold to chest)
beauty unadorned
beauty underpinned by brains
beauty's beacon
becoming
bedazzling

billet-douxable (worth sending a billet doux or love note to)
biscuit, a (attractive member of either sex)
bishoujo/bishie (*Jap.*: "beautiful girl" in manga comics lingo)
bishounen (*Jap.*: "beautiful boy" in manga comics lingo)
bodilicious, a (an alluring body)

"God made you from red clay, Flavio, with his hands. This face of yours like the little clay heads they unearth in Teotihuacán ... those eyes dark as the sacrificial wells they cast virgins into ... skin sweet as burnt-milk candy, smooth as river water."

—Sandra Cisneros, *Woman Hollering Creek*, 1991

---

bedroom-eyed
bedworthy
beef-a-roni, a (muscular male)
beguiles the eye
beguiling
belle, the
besiegingly lovely
bespanglement of beauty, a (adornment of jewels or beads)
bewitching
beyond dashing

body by Bronzino (Agnolo Bronzino, 16th-century Florentine artist)
body by Michelangelo
body by Rodin (Auguste Rodin, 19th-century French sculptor)
body by Vargas (pinup illustrator)
body by Vulcan (Roman god of fire and metalsmithing)
bona vardering (*UK*, good

looking)
bonny
bootylicious
boo-yah
born to be ogled
Botticellian
braw (fine-looking)
brilliance, a
bristling good looks
bucolic paradise (countryside)
buff/buffed (muscularly fit, well-
   toned, attractive)
buffed and burnished
call to intimacy, a
callipygian (having shapely
   buttocks)
captivating
caressable
Cary Grant 2.0
cascade of loveliness, a
case for the sense of touch, a
case for 20–20 vision, a
celestial-tantara beautiful (blast
   of trumpet)
cerulean splendor (perfect-blue
   sky)
chick gravity (attractiveness to
   women)
chick magnet, a (attractive male)
chinchilla

chiseled like Waterford glass
chong (*UK*, handsome)
chung (buff, sexy)
Circean (treacherously seductive)
Clark Gable 2.0
classy
clinquant (glittering, tinseled)
coddles the eye
come-hithering
comely
concussively beautiful
conjugation of beauty and grace,
   a
contoured (curvaceous)
conversion-worthy gorgeous
   (worth religious conversion)
coruscant (having brilliant points
   or flashes of light)
coruscatingly beautiful (giving
   off brilliant flashes of light)
criminally handsome
crystalline
dangerously handsome
darkly bewitching
dashing
David, a
D-cup zaftig/zoftig (voluptuous)
death-blow beautiful
decorous
Denzel Washington 2.0

dewdrop delicacy, a
diamond-tiara dazzling
diaphanous (finely transparent)
disarmingly lovely
dishy
disquietingly lovely (causing
    nervousness)
dolorously beautiful (achingly)
Dorothy Dandridge 2.0
double-take worthy
doubly dazzling
downy
dreamy
Dresden-china-like (exquisitely
    crafted china)
drop-dead devastating
dwells in beauty
Eden, an
eerily beautiful
effulgent (radiating brilliant
    light)
elaboration of beauty, an
elating
elegant
eleven, an (woman more perfect
    than a 10)
embraceable
embroidered in the empyrean
    (heavens)
emphatically buff

ensorcelling (bewitching)
enduringly fair
enervatingly beautiful (weaken-
    ingly)
engorgingly hot
enrapturing (moving to delight)
enravishing (enrapturing)
enshrinable
enticing
entrancing
ethereally beautiful (airily, intan-
    gibly)
euphonic/euphonious (pleasing to
    the ear)
eurhythmic (harmoniously
    ordered or proportioned)
extravagantly handsome
eye candy
eyeballs, behave!
eyeful, an
eye-mistingly beautiful/gorgeous
face by Botticelli
face by Raphael (ref., the Renais-
    sance painter Raphael)
face by Renoir
fallen from the clouds/heavens
fatally handsome
fearfully gorgeous
feathery
feline

feloniously stacked
fetching
fetchingly foxy
finely featured
finely wrought
fit (*UK*, suggesting sexual attractiveness)
flaming beautiful (*UK*)
flawlessly composed
flourish of splendor, a
forbidden-fruit alluring
fulgent (gleaming)
full-throated (of singing: deep, rich)
fulminating beauty, a (exploding)
gaga-making
gallantly handsome
gauge of beauty, the
gazelline (gazelle-like)
ginchy (wonderfully attractive)
glamazon, a (glamorous plus Amazon)
"glass of fashion and the mold of form," the (—Shakespeare, *Hamlet*, 3.1)
glistening
goddess in full, a
goddesslike
go-limp beautiful
goo-goo-eyeable

gossamer delicacy, of
got her pretty on
got his handsome on
gracefully nuanced
gracile (attractively slender, willowy)
gravitationally attractive
guapo/guapa (*Sp*.: good-looking)
guapísimo/guapísima (*Sp*.: extremely beautiful)
guy gravity (attractiveness to men)
guy magnet, a
Halle Berry 2.0
hands-off perfection
harvest-moon lovely
has beauty to burn
hauntingly fair
hazardously hot
head-turning
heart-chafingly beautiful
heart-flutteringly gorgeous
heart-impounding
heating-and-bothering beautiful
heir to Adonis, an
heiress to Aphrodite, an
Helen of Troy, a
helpless-making gorgeous
homage to beauty, a
hormone-roiling

hot and bothering
hot-blooded
hottie, a
hunky
idyllic (serenely beautiful, charm-
    ingly rural)
in blushing flower
in perfect bloom

juggernaut of beauty, a (over-
    whelming, destructive force)
Junoesque
kaleidoscopic (shifting colors or
    patterns)
killing
kippy (*CAN*, of a woman: attrac-
    tive)

"The loveliness of the day was enough to *knock you
down*."

—Wells Tower,
Everything Ravaged, Everything Burned, 2009

---

incandescent
indifferently handsome
inexcusably handsome
inordinately attractive
intricately fashioned
inviting
involute (complex, intricate, as in
    spiraled shells)
iridescent (lustrous with colors)
irksomely beautiful
irresistible
it calls to me
I've-fallen-and-I-can't-get-up
    gorgeous

kissable
kissy-huggy
knock-down lovely
knockout, a
laceratingly beautiful
lambent (effortlessly glowing or
    brilliant)
lapidary features (fine-cut, like
    gems)
lathe-turned
lavishlimbed (—James Joyce,
    *A Portrait of the Artist as a
    Young Man*)
lavishly endowed

Lena Horne 2.0
Leonardo DiCaprio 2.0
leonine
lick-her-boots seductive
Ligurian-Sea goddess, a (*ref.*, glamorous Riviera-coastal sea)
like seeing the Sistine Chapel
lithe/lissome/lithesome (beautifully graceful)
lock-me-up-and-throw-away-the-key seductive
looker, a
loomed in paradise
luminous
luminously fair
lushly beautiful
lustrous
Lydian (of music: gentle, soft, voluptuous)
magically juvenescent (becoming youthful)
mahou shoujo (*Jap.*: young female superheroes in manga comics lingo)
make-a-joyful-noise beautiful
mane of spun gold, a
manicured
manifestly handsome
manna to mine cochlea (hearing organ)

Marilyn Monroe 2.0
Marlon Brando 2.0
marmoreal (marblelike)
Matt Damon 2.0
mellifluous (sweet)
mens sana in corpore sano (*L.*: a sound mind in a sound body)
MEOW-target, a (my eyes open wide)
MEPO-target, a (my eyes pop out)
Michelangelian
model of grace, a
mohair-soft
moony-making
mortally wounding beauty, a
mossy-soft
Mozartian
must-be-a-mirage beautiful
nacreous (like iridescent mother-of-pearl)
narcotically beautiful
nebulosity of beauty, a (space cloud)
nice-nice (*UK*)
no bum for looks
no-ifs-ands-or-buts beautiful
not deficient in the looks department
not exactly repellant

not scantily endowed
not unhandsome
not unlovely
not unpleasing to the eye
nuanced loveliness, a (subtle, varied)
nubile (of a sexually mature young woman)
objet d'art, an
obliviously alluring
obsidian (intense black of volcanic glass)

out of a Renoir
panoply of colors, a (array)
pantherine (pantherlike)
paradise on earth
pellucid (maximum transparency)
Penelope Cruz 2.0
peng
phosphorescent (giving off retained light without heat)
photogenically fair
pieridine (butterflylike)

"The mix of delicacy and strength has an almost *Mozartian* quality to it, a sense of light, graceful detail applied to a firm and self-assured structure."

—Paul Goldberger of Cass Gilbert's
Woolworth Building in Manhattan.
The Skyscraper, 1983

ogle-worthy
one-woman gawker's delay, a
opalescent (milky or multicolored iridescence)
orchid-lovely
out of a da Vinci
out of a Lautrec

pinch-me perfect
pitilessly gorge (gorgeous)
poised
princely beauty, a
pristine (pure, unspoiled)
promulgation of splendor, a (declaration)

punishingly handsome
pure poetry
radiance, a
radiant
radiates from the heavens
rakishly handsome
Raphaelesque (*ref.*, the Renaissance painter Raphael)
ravages the senses
ravishing

riotously beautiful
rivetingly handsome
robustly fetching
Rock Hudson 2.0
royal-diadem worthy (royal crown)
rubberneck-worthy
Rubenesque/Rubensian (voluptuous, in the style of the painter Peter Paul Rubens)

"Three things are needed for beauty, wholeness, harmony and *radiance*."
—Thomas Aquinas via Stephen Dedalus in *A Portrait of the Artist as a Young Man*, 1916

---

recklessly handsome
reeling-feeling beautiful
refulgent (radiant)
regally attired
religious-making beauty
Renoir-beautiful
repository of beauty, a
resplendent (splendid, dazzling)
reverberatingly beautiful
rhapsodic (exaltingly expressive)
rigged-out

ruby-spangled
rugged (of a boy: rough-edged sexy)
Salma Hayek 2.0
sanguine (ruddy)
sapphirine (like sapphire)
satiny
sculptured
searching beauty, a (keen, intense)
searingly hot

sets your heart careening
shapely
she-devil fine
shockingly gorgeous
sidereal splendor, a (stellar)
Sidney Poitier 2.0
signal beauty, a
silken
sinewy
sinuous (lithe, graceful)
sirenically seductive (*ref.*, mythological deceiving beauties, the Sirens)
slaughtering
slayingly gorge (gorgeous)
sloe-eyed (dark, almond-shaped)
smiting
snow-blindingly beautiful
sonorous (producing deep, rich sound)
Sophia Loren 2.0
soul-shackling beauty
sparkling
spar-shouldered (wide support for sail)
spellful
stabbingly beautiful
starlit
star-studded
steaming

steeped in beauty
sternly handsome
stormily handsome
stretch-limo sleek/svelte
stud muffin (sexy male)
studio-star gorgeous
studly
stunner, a
stunning
stupid fine (*rap*: stupid = extremely)
sultry (suggestive of heated passion, sensuality)
supple
svelte
sweep-off-the-feet beguiling
swoll (muscled up)
sylphidine (slender, airy, graceful; of woman or girl)
sylphlike (slender, graceful of figure)
sylvan paradise (forest)
tantalizing
tear-one's-heart-out gorgeous
tenth-power gorgeous
texture of royal porcelain, a
"thing of beauty, a" (—John Keats, "Endymion," 1818)
timelessly appealing
Titianesque (*ref.*, 16th-century

Venetian painter: voluptuous)

transfixing

transgressively beautiful

Turneresque (*ref.*, English painter Joseph Turner's fluent, radiant landscapes)

Twilight-type hot (*ref.*, *The Twilight Saga* teen romances, 2005–)

twitch-makingly beautiful

un bel homme (*Fr.*: a handsome man)

unadorned beauty

unadornedly fair

unblemished

unconscionably beautiful

une belle (*Fr.*: a beautiful woman)

unembellished beauty

unfadingly handsome

unforgivably gorgeous

unhingingly handsome

unpardonably pretty

unsettlingly handsome

Valentino 2.0

vampy (seductive)

vampirically fetch

Venus de Milo with arms, a

vernal beauty, a (spring-season-like)

vicuña-soft (a rare wool)

vision, a

visual picnic, a

vividly handsome (—Janet Malcolm)

voluptuous

Vulcan-glazed (Roman god of fire)

wallopingly attractive

watch of nightingales, lovely as a

wave-the-white-flag gorgeous

well-turned

where beauty lays its head

wholesomely fair

willowy

wiltingly gorgeous

winning

winsomely dimpled

woven in heaven

wreathed in beauty

zaftig/zoftig (voluptuous)

VINTAGE GOLD*

bellafatima
buttercup, a
catchy number, a
cutie-pie, a
easy on the eyes
fetcher, a
glamour girl, a
hot puppy, a
hot stuff
hot tomato, a
hotcha
hotsy-totsy
hugsome
ohmigoddess, an
peachagulu
prize package, a
sheikish
slick article, a
stone fox, a
sweet patootie, a
swell article, a

* With its tarnish of sexism typical of earlier eras.

PERIDOT EYES, ALABASTER THIGHS, AND LAPIS LAZULI SKIES:
MINERALS FOR METAPHORS OF BEAUTY

aquamarine (sky-blue to blue-green beryl)

alabaster (white and translucent)

amber

amethyst (pale violet to rich purple quartz)

black and white onyx (banded agate chalcedony, used in cameo carvings)

bloodstone/heliotrope (green chalcedony with red spots)

blue zircon (diamond-brilliant blue)

bornite (purplish iridescence)

carnelian chalcedony (clear to translucent reddish-brown)

cinnamon stone garnet (red)

cornelian chalcedony (translucent red)

emerald

epidote (yellowish, pistachio green)

fire agate (rainbowed browns, other colors, with iridescent effects in light)

jadite/jade (pale green)

lapis lazuli (azure)

malachite (rich green)

peridot /olivine (bottle-green)

pyrope garnet (ruby red)

rhodonite (pink)

ruby

sapphire

topaz (rose-pink, sherry brown)

turquoise (robin's-egg blue)

white opal (milky white)

JOY-GIVING

* Pleasurable
* Charming
* Comforting
* Blissful
* Peaceful/Relaxing
* Renewing

PRAISE THAT KEEPS GIVING

In this section we go beyond such terms as *fun* and *pleasing*, which have their places, but are pale acclaim for the things that give us exceptional joy, comfort, and renewal.

With joyful things, there can be a whole chain of giving. A comedy gives me paroxysmal laughter; I give back by acclaiming it to others; others credit me for a night of lachrymose howls. What's not to like here?

The very compiling of this category uncorked a flight of pleasures: a list-maker's avaricious delight at sheer number—all those buried gems and fresh coinages for expressing a sentiment; an affirmation of joy's immeasurable varieties, from relief to ecstasy; and a wallow in language tailored to spread joy by acclaiming it.

What is that cringey old phrase—"Sharing is caring"? When you think about it, a heap of sharing—say, of complaints, gossip, vacation condos—has to do with self-interest. So does sharing of joy. We humans derive an odd enhancement of pleasure from acclaiming what pleases us and, even better, persuading others to experience it. But surely we can count this as a plus for our species. What if we'd evolved like spiders, hoarding joys like rolled-up flies?

Mark Twain remarked that "Grief can take care of itself; but to get the full value of a joy you must have somebody to divide it with." So there you are, straight from the man who perhaps gave more joy to readers than any American writer. And how, in the way of an exercise, might one acclaim such a person? I'm going with a quick a, b, c of choices from the list that follows: Twain is an *anti-doldrumine*, a *bacchanal for the brain*, and a *cure for blocked ch'i*.

Your turn.

TERMS

affirming joy, an
all's-well territory
amicable
amuses the eye
analeptic (invigorating)
anchorage for the soul
aneurism-inducing[ly funny]
    (—Ken Babstock, *Toronto
    Globe & Mail*)
angelus, an (bell for prayer
    commemorating the incarna-
    tion of Jesus)

antidote to a bad day, the
arousing
asylum for the spirit
auspicious (promising favorable
    outcome)
avuncular (like a good-humored
    uncle)
bacchanal for the brain, a
bacchanal, a (drunken, riotous
    party)
balm for the blues, a
balm, a

"She feels something break upon her. An *angelus* of
clearest joy...."

—Don DeLillo, *Underworld*, 1997

---

anodyne (pain-relieving,
    soothing)
anti-doldrumine, an (relieves the
    doldrums)

balsam of Mecca, a (*ref.*, healing
    resinous balm, probably balm
    of Bible)
Barnumesque

beatific (imparting bliss)
beatifying (making blessedly
  happy)
begets pure joy
bellwether of happiness, a
  (leading indicator)
belly-busting (comedy)
benefaction to humankind, a
blissville
blithe (pleasingly cheerful, but
  also indifferently carefree)
blizzard of joy, a
blues-banishing
blues-busting
blues-dispersant, a
blues-muzzling
blues-purging
boisterously funny
bolstering
bon mot, a (pleasing word)
bonhomous (having good-
  natured, pleasant manner)
boo-yah/booyakka/booyakasha!
  (*UK*, expression of delight)
bosom-warming
boy toy, a
brahma, a (something pleasing)
brain bacchanalia, a
brain candy
brain jubilee, a

brain-elevating
breath of happiness, a
breeder of joy, a
breezily charming
bubbling
bucking-up
bucolic (rural, pastoral)
Buddhistically calming
buoyant
buoyantly jovial
buoying
buster, a (pleasure-giving, excellent thing)
buzz trigger, a
cachinnatory (making for loud
  laughter)
cakewalk, a (easy thing, thus
  pleasurable)
canorous (melodious)
capacious welcome, a (ample,
  large)
caperingly cheerful
capriccio of charm, a (*ref.*,
  musical form: lively, free of
  rules, improvised)
caressable
carousal with pleasure, a
cascade of happiness, a
catchy
cause for rejoicing

charismatic (magnetic personality)
cheering
chicken soup's own chicken soup
chorogenic (—neologism by
linguist Bill Casselman:
inspires dancing)
clamorously jolly
clement (merciful, as in merci-
fully mild weather)
cockahooped (rendered crazily,
boastfully, drastically elated)
comic delirium
comic mayhem
constellation of smileys, a
consumingly joyful
convivial
convulsion-triggeringly funny
could milk a laugh out of a
turnip
courtly
cozy
crackling good fun
crowd-pleasing
cup of joy drained to the dregs, a
cup-runneth-over-ish
curative
cure for blocked ch'i, a (life
force/energy)
"deep swell of happiness, a"

(—Colum McCann, *Let the
Great World Spin*)
deliverance, a
demulcent (soothing)
dinner-bell cheering
dinner bell, a
distillation of happiness, a
docking with your inner child, a
dopamine flood in your reward
center, a
down-home charming
draught of joy with a head on
it, a
drenching of joy, a
dunking in bliss, a
ebullient (bubbling over with
enthusiasm)
ebulliently charming
ebullition of joy, an (overflow,
gush)
ecstasiating/ecstasizing (causing
ecstasy)
effervescent
effortlessly charming
elating
elevator to heaven, an
elfin (pixieish, usually charming)
elixir, an
Elysian (gives blissful pleasure or
delight)

Elysium, an (place of heavenly bliss)

embraceable

embrocation for the spirit, an (muscle- or joint-soothing lotion)

emollient (soothing, relaxing)

enchanting

enchiridion of joy, an (handbook, manual)

endearing

enriching

enthroned in the Happy Kingdom

envibing (causing good vibes, excitement)

eudaemonic (conducive to reason-based happiness)

euphoric/euphorigenic (yielding feeling of euphoria, well-being)

euphoriant (inducing or an inducer of euphoria)

evensong-mellow

exaltation, an

exalting

expansive (openly and good-naturedly communicative)

extrusion of pure charm, an

exuberant-making

feast of laughs, a

feathery feeling, a

feeling it (enjoying something)

felicitous (agreeably, pleasingly apt)

festal (befitting a gala festival)

first-kiss unforgettable

flight of doves, calming as a

flotationing

flotilla of joy, a

fountainhead of joy, a

free pass to forbidden fruit, a

frolicsome

frown-flipping

fugal harmony, a

full pour of happiness, a

fun house, a

funbelievable

gallant (courteous and attentive, as to women)

garlands the soul in bliss

gemütlich (Ger.: congenial, cozy)

gentle-wayed (—Colum McCann, Let the Great World Spin)

gets you jazzed (excited)

giddy-making

gift horse, mouth and all, a

gift of the Muses, a

girdingly sensual (embracingly)

glad tiding, a

glad tidings
gladdening
gladsome
gleeful
glib (offhandedly engaging, but
    sometimes insincerely so)
gloom dispersant, a
gloom-dispelling
gloomicide, a
gloom-piercing
gloom-shattering
gloom-splintering
glubbed out (*Par.*, *NZ*, relaxed)
good from knob to knickers (*UK*,
    head to underwear)
good from pate to po-po (head
    to rump)
goombah-in-need, a (*I.dialect*:
    friend)
got soul
go-tell-it-on-the-mountain good
    news
gregarious (company-seeking;
    sociable)
groove-restoring
gumbo of charms, a
halcyon/halcyonic (free of care)
hangar full of happy, a
happiness unleashed
happiness with interest

happy ending, a
happy hour, a
happy place, a
happy portent, a
Happy Valley
happy-go-larky
happy machine, a
happy-place express, a
harbinger of joy, a
harem of happy virgins, a
harem of horny virgins, a
harmonious
harvest of joy, a
heady
healing
heart-soddening (saturating the
    heart)
high-functioning entertainment
    machine, a (—Mick LaSalle,
    San Francisco Chronicle)
hoggishly pleasurable
hogshead of joy, a (big barrel)
homey, a (trusted, fond friend)
hoped-for
hospitable
hymnal of joyful song, a
hype (fun, wild, rowdy)
idyllic (ideally perfect, peaceful,
    charming)
illuminating

in your oils (*Par.*, delighted)

inamorato/a, an (loved one; lover)

incapacitatingly funny

incubation of pleasure, an (hatching)

infatuating

infectious

infectiously upbeat

infusion of joy, an

infusion of mirth, an

inhumanly funny

inner-space salve, an

inoculation of joy, an

insouciant (cheerfully absent of worries)

irenic (promoting peace)

itch-scratchingly satisfying

jaunty

jocund (jolly)

jollification, a

jollying

joy bank, a

joy by the gigabyte

joy express, a

joy missile, a

joy-launcher, a

joy without dimension, a

joyously anticipated

joy-spreading

jubilation, a

jubilating

kicked back (relaxed)

killing (wildly affecting)

kissy-huggy

klutzily delightful

knell of joy, a

lachrymosely funny (tearily)

lachrymosely joyous

lambastingly funny

landfall of bliss, a

larky (merry, carefree; of playful, innocent mischief)

lather of bliss, a

lathering (exciting)

laugh-launching

laughquake, a

lenitive, a (mitigating, soothing—but also laxative)

levitating

licky-face

life in Cockaigne (imaginary land of luxury and plenty)

life preserver, a

light at the end of the wormhole, the

light-spreading

Ligurian Sea of bliss, a (glamorous Riviera-coastal sea)

lilt, a (light, tripping song)

liltingly cheering

limped-out (relaxed)

lodestone of blessings, a (has strong magnetic quality)

longed-for

lucre for the soul (money)

ludic (playful)

magnetic

makes-your-heart-go-hardy-har-har

melancholy-buster, a

mellifluous (smooth-flowing, sweet)

mirage made real, a

mirthful

"moist balsamic breath, a" (—Thomas Mann, *The Magic Mountain*)

mollifying (mood-softening, pacifying, soothing)

moorings for the troubled mind

mud-in-your-eye moment, a

muse-charming

muse-inspired

neighborly

nepenthean (worry-freeing; from nepenthe, ancient anti-grief drug)

nirvanic (setting the soul free of pain)

not inauspicious (not disallowing a favorable outcome)

not infelicitous (not failing to be pleasingly apt)

not unpropitious (not unfavorable)

not untimely

not-a-dry-seat-in-the-house hilarious

on cloud nine

operatic crescendo of joy, an

opportune (advantageous)

orgasmathon, an

orgasmic

orgy of delights, an

over-the-moon elating

over-the-top funny

oxygenation, an

paid furlough, a

paid vacation, a

palliative, a

panacean (curing all)

paradise on earth

paroxysmally funny (causing violent onset of symptoms)

pawky (*SCOT*, dryly witty)

pecker-buoying (*UK*, spirit-lifting)

pelf for the spirit (money)

perfect storm of pleasures, a

personable

picturesque

pitter-pattering of hope, a

pixieish

pizzazzical (having pizzazz)

placid

playful

pleasantly evocative

pleasantly pashy (passionate)

pleasure garden for the mind, a

pleasure lode, a

pluviosity of pleasure, a (rainfall)

po-po-warming

prayer-answering

prepossessing (presenting attractive or pleasing impression)

prime roast on your platter

progenitor of joy, a (begetter)

propitious (favorable)

psychic dividend, a

psychic pelf (money)

pure Attic simplicity (pared elegance)

pure honey

rallying

rapturous

ray of bliss, a

rebuttal to boredom, a

redeeming

red-letter (joyful or festive, as in red-letter day)

regalement, a (sumptuous entertainment or feast)

regales the spirit (provides sumptuous joy)

regaling (providing sumptuous joy)

regenerating

regenerative

rejoinder to despair, a

renewing

restorative

reviving

revivifying

reviviscent

rewarding

rhapsody, a (exuberant, impassioned expression)

riant (laughingly cheerful, mirthful)

risible (ridiculously funny; causing laughter)

roborant, a (strengthening tonic)

romantic turbulence, a

romping (exciting)

rosy

rousing

rush of gaiety, a

rush, a

sadness solved

safe harbor
safe house for the soul, a
safe house for the spirit, a
salad days redux (youthful inno-
	cence brought back)
saltant joy (leaping, dancing)
salubrious (favorable to health
	and well being)
salvational
salve, a
sanctuary for the soul, a
sanctuary for the spirit, a
sanctum sanctorum, a (private
	refuge from everyday concerns)
saturnalia, a (wild celebration,
	revelry; orgiastic at its wildest)
Saturnian (happy, prosperous,
	peaceful)
scintillating/scintillant (spar-
	kling; pleasingly witty)
score! (shout expressing joy)
sedating
seizure! (*Par.*, *UK*, cry of any
	small triumph)
seizure-inducingly funny
sensual (arousing)
serene
serenely pastoral
seven-happiness mashup, a
shanti for the soul (peace, Hindu)

shuttle to paradise, a
simpatico (congenial)
slaphappy (pleasantly giddy or
	silly)
slaying (hilarious)
slick (appealing, charming)
snug harbor, a
spankingly amusing
spiky
spirit-lifting
spiritual fiesta, a
spiritual *schvitz*, a (*Yi.*: sweat
	bath)
spiritual shoring up, a (propping
	up)
spiritual spa, a
sprightly
springlike
springtide of joy, a
springy
spritz of joy, a
Steinway sound, a
storm shelter, a
Stradivarian sweetness, a (*ref.*,
	Stradivarius violins)
succor
sulk-dispelling
sunny
susurration of joy, a (whisper)
sweet haven, a

sweet refuge

sylvan

syrup for the soul

taproot of contentment, the

thaumaturge, a (worker of miracles or magic)

third wind, the (euphoric goal of extreme aerobics)

three-ply charming

tickles the spirit

tickling

tiene duende (*Sp.*: has a magical, inspired charm)

Tiggerish (*ref.*, Tigger of *Winnie the Pooh*: cheerful, irrepressible)

tintinnabulation of joy, a (bell-ringing)

titillating

Tivoli for the soul (*ref.*, Danish amusement park)

tonic, a

touch of eros, a

tranquil

transporting

trip to Happy Valley, a

tumescence of joy, a

tumultuously passionate

ululatingly funny (howlingly)

unaffectedly charming

unbearably erotic

"unbodied joy" (—Percy Bysshe Shelley, "To a Skylark")

unendurably arousing

unfettered bliss

upful (*JAM*, cheerful, positive)

uptown Eden

uptown paradise

uptown Xanadu (imaginary place of luxury and magnificence)

vade mecum of happiness, a (*L.*: handbook)

va-va-voom (exciting, vigorous, attractive)

verspertinely peaceful (evening time)

voyage to paradise, a

waggish

walking hymn, a

warmly enveloping

weapon of mass delectation, a

weightless happiness, a

welling of joy, a

well-making

wellspring of peace, a

whalesong-serene

where troubles vaporize

whimsically playful

will make your blood do a buck jump (bucking horse jump)

will make your bones boogie

will make your heart do a
  capriole (playful leap, as by
  show horse)

will make your heart do a High-
  land fling

will make your heart leapfrog

will make your heart pole-vault

will make your heart warble

will make your soul cut a caper

will make your soul hip-hop

winsome (charming in an innocent, sometimes childlike way)

wished for and welcome

wit that could sharpen pencils

womby

wreathes the soul in joy

Wüsthof-sharp witted (premium
  kitchen knife)

yin and yang in harmony (cool/
  dark/passive and hot/bright/
  aggressive forces)

zingy

"To be concealed, protected, guarded, that is all I have
ever truly wanted, to burrow down into a place of *womby*
warmth...."

—John Banville, *The Sea*, 2005

VINTAGE GOLD

boop-boop-a-dooper, a
bricky
cutup, a
ding-dong daddy, a
funster, a
gasser, a
good time Charlie, a
high-kicker, a
jammy
ladylove, a
main squeeze, a
peppy
pert
rapteriferous
roritorious
whoop-it-upper, a

LARGE

* Huge
* Many
* Abundant
* Abounding
* Capacious
* Overflowing
* Deep

IT'S ALL RELATIVE

How big is "large"? It depends. Are you asking Atlas the Titan bearing the heavens on his shoulders, or an amoeba dodging zooplankton? If you ask me, I consider six-footers to be large, SUVs enormous, and my property tax hefty—and I need no special superlatives to make the point.

Outside such mundane items, however, loom phenomena too great in size or amount to distinguish with the usual synonyms of "big." *Huge*, *gigantic*, and *tremendous* may suit the advertisers of Black Friday bargains, but oversized vermin, half-billion-cubic-meter dams, and cosmic reaches demand more forceful (or more specific) modifiers. We want to distinguish the bigness of something (*cloud-piercing*, *epical*); we want our experience with the thing to be impressive (a *growler-full* of beer); we want to exaggerate for the sake of storytelling, humor, or sales (a *tyrannosaurian* cockroach, a *cathedralesque* dining room); or we want to amplify bigness with the force of unorthodox expression (*bookoo*, *stonking huge*, *from hell to breakfast*).

The most overwhelmingly big things in our lives—structures, natural objects, cosmic phenomena—challenge our language of acclaim; often we describe them by what they do: *skyscraping*, *thundering*, *atom-splitting*, *earthshaking*, *time-warping*. But the things themselves give us metaphors for acclaiming (or hyping) the bigness of other phenomena: *Mastodonic* proportions. *Oceanic* amounts. *A Niagara* of tears. *A Great Wall* of waste.

To get away from clichés, one can choose from hundreds of recorded immensities and make one's own metaphors. A favorite example is Martin Amis's use of the *Mahabharata*—a Hindu epic of thousands of couplets—to convey the dimensions of "a Mahabharata of pain." Ideally such references should be familiar to or made familiar to one's audience, but sometimes the weight of the words themselves imply bigness: *Brobdingnagian*, from the race of giants in *Gulliver's Travels*; *Chomolungman*, after the Tibetan name for Mt. Everest; *Burj Khalifan*, referring to the (latest) world's tallest building. You want vast? How about an *Eyjafjallajökull* of an ash cloud, recalling the one that spread from that Icelandic volcano across Europe and Asia in spring 2010.

Often, nothing can acclaim bigness like understatement, allowing the imagination to adjust for modesty or irony. How much money did so-and-so give away last year? Let's just say "it was not unsubstantial."

Superlarge numerical terms—millions, trillions—seem to have lost their figurative power in acclaiming bigness. While a million bucks sounds good to most of us as pocket money, the amount deflates in figures of speech like "I already told you a million times," or "It's a million miles from downtown." Our need for impressive numbers has given rise to such infantile but amusing inventions as *jillion*, *squillion*, *bazillion*, and *gazillion*, with sounds that can be uttered emphatically. A *googol*, or 1 followed by 100 zeros, was a handy term for exaggeration until Google the enterprise swallowed it whole. A *googolplex* still serves to stun the mind: it is 10 to the googol power—or so I learned via Google.

TERMS

abysmal
abyssal
abyssal plain, an (vast deep-ocean plain)
all-embracing
all-pervading
archipelago, an
argosy, an (large ship, fleet, or supply)
"armada of Homeric proportions, an" (—Ben Macintyre, *Operation Mincemeat*)
astronomic
avalanchine
bankrolled
battalions of
bazillion, a
beyond big
beyond copious
beyond Guinness records
beyond mammoth
beyond massive
Big Dig, a (*ref.*, Boston's massive tunnel project)

Big-Muddy big (Mississippi River)
big-rig big (*ref.*, tractor trailer, eighteen-wheel and above)
blank check, a
boa gulp, a
bookoo (for beaucoup: a large number of)
boundless
bountiful
bounty of, a
Brobdingnagian (*ref.*, race of giants in *Gulliver's Travels*)
brontosaurian
bubble on a boom, a (swollen economy)
bull moose, a (big, powerful man)
bumper crop, a
Burj Khalifan (*ref.*, Burj Khalifa, world's tallest building, 2010)
burly
by the bargeload
by the tanker full

canyon, a
caravans of
carloads
cataclysmic
cathedralesque
cavernous
chasmal (chasmlike)
Chomolungman (*ref.*, Chomol-
ungma, Tibetan name for Mt.
Everest)
clinically oversized

cosmically spacious
crater, a
crazy large
cyclonic
Dead Sea Depression, a (lowest
land elevation)
deepwater-rig deep (*ref.*, miles-
deep offshore oil wells)
defies calculation
dinosaurian
dirty huge

"There were hotels so large other hotels could have checked into them."
—Will Self, *The Book of Dave*, 2006

---

cloud-capped
cloud-piercing
coliseum, a
Colossus-of-Rhodes awesome
(*ref.*, Ancient Wonder towering
statue)
constellation, a (group of stars in
a pattern)
continental-shelf-sized
cornucopia, a (abundant source)
cosmic

double elephant folio, a (*ref.*,
largest book size, to 50 inches
tall)
epical
epidemic
Everest, an
expanding-universe size
extragalactic
extraterrestrial reach, an
extravagance, an
extravaganza, an

fathomless (bottomless, impossible to determine depth)

fifty-eleven (slang for big number)

filthy great (*UK*, extremely large)

first magnitude, of the

from hell to breakfast (from one end of the earth to the other)

from here to the back of beyond

from here to the exosphere (peak of the atmosphere)

galactic

gargantuan

gazillion, a

giant-sequoia-sized

gigabig

gigantesque

jillion, a (vast millions)

glacial

global

gobs of

God-size

Godzillian

gone rampant

goodly

goozle, a (great amount)

great muchness, a

Great Wall of China, a

grillion, a

growed-up truck, a (*Par.*, eigh-teen-wheeler)

growler-full, a (pail or other large beer container)

gulf, a

hangar-sized

hardly a mite

hardly inconsiderable

hardly meager

heaven-reaching

heavyweight

heroic

high roller, a

high-stakes

Himalayan (*ref.*, the Himalayan Mountains or Himalayas)

hippopotamic

hogshead and a half, a (big barrel)

hyas (*CAN*, big)

hyiu (*CAN*, many, much)

hyper

immeasurable

imposing

incalculably large

incomprehensible immensity, an

inestimable (beyond estimation)

inexhaustible

infinite

infinitude, an

interstellar leap, an

juggernaut, a (large overwhelming, often cruel, force)
landslides of
Large-Hadron-Collider large
(ref., world's largest particle
accelerator)
leagues of
legions of
leviathan (whale-sized)
lifty
light years
litter of, a
looming
lunker, a (something large for its
kind, usually a game fish)
mad huge
magnitudinous
magnum, a (1.5-liter bottle for
alcoholic beverage)
Mahabharata, a (ref., voluminous epic poem of India)
Mahabharata-length (ref., epic
poem of India)
majestic
majuscules, in (large letters)
mammoth
mammoth-assed
mansional
masses
masses of muchness

massif, a (mountain mass)
mastodonic
megajumbo
megamonstrous
millioni (mock Italian for
millions)
moby (whale-ishly large and
unwieldy)
Moby Dick-sized
monarch of the forest (tall tree)
mondo
mongo
monster-truck size
monumental
morbidly huge
more than somewhat (—Damon
Runyan)
multifarious (including many
different elements)
nebula/nebulosity, a (ref., region
or cloud of interstellar dust
and gas)
nebular
nimiety, a (large amount, more
than needed)
no meager amount
not a pittance
not exactly a smidgeon
not inadequate
not piddling

not unsubstantial
oceanic
Olympian (cloud-height;
    surpassing; of Olympics
    quality)
operatic
ozone-hole-sized opening, an
pachydermous (elephantlike)
pack-ice sprawl, a (*ref.*, large area
    of sea ice)
palatial
panoramic
pendulously weighty
planetal (like a planet)
plenitude, a (abundance)
plenitudinous

puts up some Brett Favre
    numbers
puts up some Kobe Bryant
    numbers
puts up some Michael Jordan
    numbers
puts up some Nolan Ryan
    numbers
Pyramidal
pythonine (pythonlike)
quantum catapult, a (significant,
    sudden leap or advance)
raft of, a
rambling
replete with (amply supplied)
sea sands, the

"It was not, however, a matter of a few miserable drops
of rain. There were bucketfuls, jugfuls, whole niles,
iguaçús, and yangtses of the stuff ..."
    —José Saramago, *Seeing*, 2006

---

plenteous (abundant)
plethora, a (superabundance,
    overabundance)
polar cap, a
prodigious

serious avoirdupois (weight)
seventy-two-point type (large
    type size)
sheaves of
shedful, a

sink hole, a
skadoodles of
skyscraping
slathers of
slew, a
smothering of, a
space beyond dimension
space-warpingly vast
spectacular
spectacular, a
sprawling
squillion, a
stack, a
stackloads of
stadium-sized
steroidally bulked
stonking huge (*UK*)
strapping
summitless
superabundance, a
supernova, a (immensely powerful, bright stellar explosion)
superstratum of all superstrata, the (top layer of all layers)
supertanker, a
tankard-sized swig, a
tankful, a
telephone numbers of money (7–10 figures)

teravolt or two, a (teravolt = one million million volts)
thousand big ones, a (million dollars)
Three Gorges Dam, a (*ref.*, vast Chinese dam system)
time-warpingly distant
Titanic
to the far reaches
to the utmost/uttermost boundaries
tornadic
towering
train of miles, a
triple-XL (clothing size)
tumultuous (crowd-strength riotous, upheaving)
tyrannosaurian
unbounded
universe of, a
unquantifiably immense
untolds (*AUSTRAL*)
uttermost, the
Van Allen Belt, a (*ref.*, radiation bands around Earth)
"vast of heaven, the" (—John Milton)
voluminous
walloping
whacking large (*UK*)

whole kingdom and phylum, the
world of, a
worldwide

VINTAGE GOLD

doozie, a
Gogmagotical (*ref.*, mythic British giant Gogmagog)
kiss-sky (tall)
mickle (many)
myriadfold
oodles
roomly
scads
squidgy
swopping
umpteen
whang-dilly

STUFFED TO BURSTING:
THE PORTMANTEAU

When the going gets big, describers reach for a superlative with the sound and weight of bigness. Standard words failing, they can consider the portmanteau: parts of two or more loaded words blended into one. Some portmanteaus made it into our main lists, but most of them tend toward the inane or juvenile—more suitable for playful use than cerebral essays. Still, a silly word can have the heft of a boa that has swallowed two pigs. Here are 12 such. If you're sufficiently bodacious (bold + audacious) you can invent your own.

abnormous
cornucopious
gargantanic
gigental
ginormous
grandacious
grandificent
hugeous
humongous
jumbonomic
monstracious
monstropolous

EXCEPTIONAL

* **Extraordinary**
* **Different**
* **Rare**
* **Awesome**
* **Unique**

RESERVED FOR ONE OF A KIND

What is "exceptional"? Think of a popular figure who towers above others in the same field, or a writer whose primacy is unchallenged, or a place like no other.

Let's say you thought of Oprah Winfrey, William Shakespeare, and Venice. What terms of acclaim would suit them? Various words and phrases listed under "Great" might do the job; but if you wanted to imply singular greatness, uniqueness, or rarity, the suggestions in this category would take you in that direction.

Oprah fans, for example, might praise her as *iconic* or *the queen bee*. Shakespeare? *Peerless. All-eclipsing.* Venice could lay claim to being *sui generis* or "of its own kind," in a class by itself.

Some things win acclaim for being amusingly or courageously exceptional, if not universally esteemed. Terms such as *edgy*, *fringey*, and *gonzo* might apply. A college roommate of mine had a unique talent of perching, squirrel-like, on fence posts and other coaster-sized elevated platforms. *Bizarro*, perhaps?

Because varied phenomena, not just the rarest and most extraordinary, can inspire awe, the word *awesome* pops up within other categories in this book; but I've featured it here to underscore its natural association with exceptional things. The term has historically acclaimed things that inspire fear or reverence. After some 500 years, however, it has been so devalued by application to the unexceptional that it must be intensified to carry any force. To juice it up I've employed such devices as metaphor, personification, and Germanisms, as in *an avalanche of awesome*, *awesome on stilts*, and *fall-to-your-knees awesome*. Such terms are best reserved for the Machu Picchus and Halley's Comets in our lives and not for foot-long sandwiches—unless stuffed with truffles and caviar.

TERMS

abnormal
all-eclipsing
ambrosia amid Kool-Aid
antithesis of ordinary, the
atypical
avalanche of awesome, an
avant-garde (at the forefront; daring, unorthodox)
awe-inspiring
awesome embodied
awesome on stilts
awesome run amok
awesome unabridged
bail <u>out</u>! (as in "shut <u>up</u>!" meaning "extraordinary news!")
beyond the event horizon (boundary in space beyond which nothing can affect an observer)
big-bang awesome
bizarre
bizarro
black swan, a (an extraordinary, unexpected event, like a black swan bred of whites)
blessing of unicorns, rare as a
blow-the-bugle awesome
bomb, the
breakaway
buckaroo
Cadillac
cast in its own mold
caviar
certified rare
class of the field, the (as in best rated for a horse race)
clear <u>out</u>! (as in "shut <u>up</u>!" meaning "extraordinary news!")
come-outer, a (dissenter from a group)
contrarian, a
cruise ship among dinghies, a
daringly different
Day-Glo against dun
diamond of the first water, a (top grade)

different drummer, a
dissenting voice, a
edgy
emerald among M&Ms, an
ermine amid mouse fur
exclamation-point exceptional
eximious (distinguished, select,
    eminent)
extraordinary underscored
extraterrestrial
fall-to-your-knees awesome
free-spirited
fringey
gender-bending (breaking gender
    stereotypes)
genre-bending /busting (breaking
    limitations of a genre)
genius emeritus
genuine article, the
giga-awesome
gonzo
got flava (has distinctive stylish-
    ness)
grizzly among teddy bears, a
hands-down different
happy aberration, a
happy mutation, a
Havana-leaf premium
icon, an (subject of veneration,
    devotion; an idol)

iconic
iconoclast, an (attacker of vener-
    ated ideas and tradition)
iconoclastic
indie
in toto awesome
industrial-strength awesome
inimitable (cannot be imitated)
irreiterable (occurring only once)
irreplaceable
its own golden rule
judderingly awesome (vibrat-
    ingly)
judderingly novel (vibratingly)
Katie-bar-the-door awesome
kiss-the-hem-of-its-robe
    awesome
kiwi, the
Lamborghini (distinctive luxury
    motor car)
log off! (as in "shut up!" meaning
    "extraordinary news!")
Louisville Slugger among
    broomsticks, a (*ref.*, premium
    baseball bat)
mansion amid hovels, a
maverick, a (nonconformist, one
    of a kind, unbranded)
Medal-of-Freedom caliber
Medal-of-Honor caliber

mediocrity cleft and sundered
Mercedes
meta-awesome
miracle of the millennium, a
monotypic (being the only
   member or representative of its
   group)
mother lode of awesome, a
mouth-gapingly awesome
muffin, the
museum-quality
Nobel-quality
normality on a toot
not normative
not white bread
off the beaten path
off the grid
offbeat
one and only, the
one of a kind, a
one-off, the (*Par.*, *UK*, unique

thing, individual, or event)
onliest, the (1581 usage, and
   contemporary slang)
ordinary cleft and sundered, the
original, an
OTT (over the top)
outsider, an
out of this universe
out-of-the-ballpark awesome
pan-awesome
paranormal
pearl before the swinish, a
peerage among peasantry
peerless
phenomenal
Piaget
pioneering
preterhuman (outside or beyond
   human)
preternatural (outside nature;
   beyond natural)

"The metaphysical explanation is that Roger Federer is one of those rare, *preternatural* athletes who appear to be exempt, at least in part, from certain physical laws … —a type that one could call genius, or mutant, or avatar."

—David Foster Wallace,
New York Times Play Magazine, August 20, 2006

queen bee, the

rara avis (*L*.: literally "rare bird": exceptional person)

rare breed, a

rarefied (elite; purged of the tasteless)

real deal, the

recherché (uncommon, exquisite; ultra-refined)

rhythmic swirl of awesomeness, a (—Alex Hamburger on contra dancing, "All Things Considered," NPR, July 10, 2010)

ruby among garnets, a

rum (odd, strange; sometimes dangerous)

salient (striking, noticeable within its context)

shiver-me-timbers awesome

shove off! (as in "shut up!" meaning "extraordinary news!")

signal

sine qua non, the (the element giving something its essence)

singular

six-layered special

startler, a

stereotype-busting

Stradivarian (rare and precious, like the famed violins)

sui generis (*L*.: of its own kind, unique)

surreal

tera-awesome (10^{12} awesome)

tertium quid of rare and awesome, a (related to but distinct from; a third thing)

three-hooters/three-ballocks exceptional

Tiffany

to cut to the chase, unique

traded-my-cat-for-a-unicorn good (—Drex D on Yelp.com)

trailblazing

transmundane (extending beyond this physical world)

truffles among toadstools

unalloyed goods, the

unchecked awesome

uncommon

uncontested

unconventional

unearthly

unheard of

unique

unorthodox

unparalleled

unstrung and over the top

unthought-of
unvarnished goods, the
unwonted (unusual, uncommon)
ur- of all ur-, the (the earliest,
    original)

vanguard
wall-to-wall awesome
whole other drumbeat, a

VINTAGE GOLD

alonely
Arabian bird, an (Phoenix, a one-of-a-kind person)
nonesuch/nonsuch
off the wall
one in a million
oner, a (one-er)
only pebble on the beach, the
seldseen
somethin' else
uncome-at-able
uncompeered
unoverpassable

A NEELANJALI RUBY AMONG GARNETS:

RARE GEMS TO DANGLE AS METAPHORS

Chloe Diamond (round brilliant-cut giant)

Cullinan Diamond (largest rough-gem-quality stone ever found)

Darya-ye-Noor Diamond (largest pink)

Gachala Emerald (one of largest)

Golden Jubilee Diamond (largest faceted ever cut)

Hope Diamond (largest deep blue)

Mogul Emerald (one of largest)

Neelanjali Ruby (largest double-star ruby)

Oppenheimer Diamond (among largest uncut gem-quality)

Star of India Sapphire (largest, most famous star)

Tiffany Yellow Diamond, a (rare of its cut variety)

Wittelsbach Blue Diamond (sold for $24.3 million in 2008)

INTENSE

* Profound
* Tense
* Serious
* Authentic
* True
* Real

STRETCHED TO THE EXTREME

The word *intense*, derived from Latin and French terms meaning "strained" or "stretched tight," now conveys not only the sense of being stretched to an extreme degree, as in *taut*, but also tightly focused or concentrated. Applied to emotions, it means extremely strong and deep, as in "intense happiness." The word is rarely used lightly, although it enjoyed a run as a synonym for "extremely cool" (That ride was *intense*, man!)

Here we stretch our "Intense" category to include what might be called extreme reality and extreme truth; that is, reality beyond foggy perceptions and truth beyond "truthiness." These sought-after qualities deserve more convincing acclaim than *totally real*, *really true*, or *absolutely true*. Our alternatives—ranging in diction from *incontrovertible* to *trill*—may strain at times, but only in the good cause of intensifying intensity.

Many of our terms address the question "How intense?" or "To what extreme degree?" How intense was that weeklong meditation retreat in Big Sur? *Allsubsuming*, *dharmic*, *reverberant*, and *brain-debugging*, one might say. One can also ratchet up the degree of intensity with forceful imagery: A literary work is *tooth-and-talons gripping*; a debate, *trench-warfare intense*; a sermon, *tunnel-drill penetrating*. If such imagery cannot be torqued to the limit to form an extreme adverb, it can usually be couched in a comparative metaphor. How intense was my first tumble into lovesickness? *Like an intercontinental ballistic missile to the gut.*

TERMS

absorbing
acute
acutely serious
airtight
alight with truth
analytical
anchored in reason
arabesque (complex, intertwined)
arresting
astringent (binding, penetrating,
    sharp)
attentive
awakening
axiomatic
bang-on-the-money (exact)
bang-to-rights evident
bankable truth, a
basso-profundo deep
bedrock
bench-vise gripping
benthic (deep)
Biblical weight, of
big as life and twice as real
biting
black-is-white epiphany, a

bleeding-edge
blinding truth, the
bona fide
boomingly true
boot-in-the-face intense
bottom line, the
bottomless
brinkish
brinky
bristling
bum-clenchingly tense
bunker-busting revelation, a
buzz-saw incisive
carved-in-stone true
case-closed final
caught-in-the-headlights reality
chain-saw cleaving
chimingly clear
clangorously real
clarified of bias ("solids"
    removed to make clear)
clenching
climacteric, a (critically impor-
    tant event or era; also meno-
    pause)

climactic

climax, the

compellingly true

concentrated

conclusive

congestion of evidence, a

consequential

consuming

contusively real (bruisingly)

convulsing

critical

deflagration, a (intensely hot, burning)

dharma incarnate (cosmic essence manifested)

dharmic (of the essential nature of the cosmos or one's self)

dialed-in (intensely focused)

distilled to its essence

drainingly intense

dredgingly poignant

edgy

"It was an earthquake, a *climacteric*, a revelation."
—Christopher Hitchens, *Hitch-22*, 2010

---

crucial

crunch time, the (critical moment)

crunking (intensely wild and exciting)

crux of the matter

crux, the

dangerous

dead-bang true

dead-on

decisively so

deep-rooted

electric

engaging

engraved in memory

engrossing

enthralling

entrenched

enveloping

eviscerating

fair dinkum/dinky-di! (*AUSTRAL*, genuine, true, righteous)

fangs-in-the-neck intense

fast-laner, a
fathomless (bottomless, impos-
    sible to determine depth)
feet-to-the-fire intense
fiercely imagined (—Michiko
    Kakutani)
flash of truth, a
frenetically wrought (feverishly,
    hurriedly done)
full-frontal
full-out
full-spectrum
furilla (*rap*: for real)
galvanic (jolting)
gen, the (genuine truth)
genuine
genuine article, the
genuine to his/her genes
gimlet-eyed (eyes penetrate and
    notice everything)
girded for action
girdingly intense (as if belting in)

gospel
go-to-the-wall guy/girl, a
grappling-iron hooking
grave
graven in stone
gravidly meaningful (pregnantly)
gravitas (*L.*: seriousness, weighti-
    ness of subject or demeanor)
gripping
guns-drawn serious
gut-level
hammer-and-tongs intense
hardly unfounded
hardly weightless
harrowing
heads-up truth, the
heavyweight
Hegelian (*ref.*, German philoso-
    pher George Wilhelm Friedrich
    Hegel)
high-wire
honed

"The complexity of this [sports-figure] scandal, the depth
of psychological and emotional trauma that must have
been and may still be present to enable it, is of *Hegelian*
dimensions."

—Matthew DeBord, The Huffington Post,
December 17, 2009

hooking

hyaline clarity, of (glassily translucent)

immersing

impenetrable

incisive

incomprehensively profound

incontestable

incontrovertible

indelible

inherently true

intensely purposed

intent (strongly attentive)

intent on (set on)

intently

in-the-trenches intense

inviolable

in-your-face real

in-your-kisser reality

ironbound conviction, an

ironclad

iron-grip intense

irreducibly true

irrefutable

jake (honest, proper, upright)

keen

kernel, pith, and sap, the

kernel, the

King James version, the (most
authentic)

knife-edged

knock-down, drag-out intense

Koranic weight, of

lapidary (concise and polished)

legit (short for legitimate)

light, the

like a submarine-killer rocket to
your cortex

like an air-to-air missile through
your head

like an intercontinental ballistic
missile to your gut

locked-down factual

loked out (performing "loco" or
wildly irrational actions)

lucidly true

Lucite-clear

manifestly true

meta- (*prefix:* beyond, after,
within, superior)

metareal (reality existing beyond
psychological subjective
perspective)

mind-debugging

mind-maulingly intense

Mishnaic density, of (*ref.,*
commentaries subset of
Talmudic Jewish law)

mordant (incisive, trenchant;
satirically biting)

mortal-lock cinch, a (sure bet)
nailed down
ne plus ultra, the (*L.*: most
    profound degree, as of a
    quality)
nerves-in-a-blender intense
no con, swindle, or flim-flam
no confusion, illusion, or hallu-
    cination
no exaggeration, mirage, or
    subterfuge

on-the-ground reality
onto the mental gangplank
    (—Dwight Garner: daring
    thought area)
open-kimono factual (nothing
    hidden, full disclosure)
out-front
paladin of truth, a (defender,
    champion)
palpable (capable of being physi-
    cally felt, as tension might be)

"He looked me in the eyes and his whispered words
emerged through a slitlike aperture, as if they were
scalpel-sharp communication wafers."
    —Roberto Bolaño, *Amulet*, 2006

no fudge, flam, or finagle
no hoax, bluff, or bamboozle-
    ment
no-joker-in-the-deck
not exactly diddly-squat
not trifling
nub, the
on point (alert and ready for
    challenging action)
on the brink
on the up-and-up

palpably true
penetrating
perfervid (extremely impas-
    sioned)
perspicacious (deeply perceptive
    and discerning)
piercing
pincering
pivotal
plein-air pure/real (*ref.*, outdoor
    light)

plumb true

poetic fire

precisely so

primal

primordial essence (original, fundamental)

probing

proven pudding, the

psyched

pukka (authentic, genuine)

pulsating

pungent

quintessential (representing the pure essence of something)

rabbinically intense

rasa, the (emotional essence or flavor of art in Hindu aesthetics)

razor-edged

real deal, the

real to the core

real to the nucleus

real to the pith and marrow

reality in the buff

reality unsnarled

reasoned truth

recondite (understandable only by experts)

reel to reel (*rap*: very real)

resounding

reverberant

scarehead, the (huge headline, often sensational)

searching

sedge of cranes, startling as a

shuddery

sitting in the crosshairs (of a weapon's eyepiece)

slammingly real

slap-honest truth, the

sleep-depriving

slippery declivity, a (slope)

soul-dredging

spot-on truth, the

spring-clamp gripping

staringly apparent

stark

starkers real (nakedly)

steep!

stomach-squooshingly tense

stone-ground truth, the

straight from the tap

straight from the tea leaves

straight puda, the (complete truth)

straight skinny, the

straight-up-and-down true

sum and substance, the

swept-up

take-it-to-the-bank certain

Talmudic authority, of (*ref.*, body of Jewish law)

Tao, the (way, ultimate reality)

taut

telling

tension you couldn't crowbar

three-stage pulse-booster, a

thrill ride, a

thuddingly true

tochis-over-teakettle (*Yi.*: *tochis* = posterior: intensely)

Tonga-Trench deep (*ref.*, 35,702-foot-deep Pacific trench)

tooth-and-talons gripping

torqued to the limit

tow-cable taut

traumatizing

trenchant

trench-warfare intense

trill (*rap*: true and real)

truculently devout (savagely)

truth hermetically sealed

truth untangled

truthburst, a

tunnel-drill penetrating

unalloyed goods, the

unarguable

unerringly true

unfathomable (depth beyond understanding)

unflinching truth, the

unshakeable truth, the

unshatterably true

unvarnished goods, the

veracious (accurate, truthful)

visceral

vivid

Wagnerian

way, the

wearing his/her game face (intense, competitive demeanor)

weighty

well grounded

what-you-see-is-what-you-get authentic

white-knuckled

wholly immersive

will cudgel your doubts

will debug your brain

winched to the limit

wired

word is bond (*rap*: telling the absolute truth)

word of the rishis, the (*ref.*, divine scribes of revelation, Hinduism)

word that (*rap*: true)

word! (true!)

wrenching

INTENSIFYING COLORS

Superlative colors are intensely affecting colors, not necessarily the confectionary hues of a digital image. In verbal expression, a little work with fresh modifiers, metaphors, or other figures of speech can produce colors as emotionally intense as any pumped-up pixels. Some examples:

"hectic red"—Percy Bysshe Shelley, "Ode to the West Wind"

"seismically red"—Diane Ackerman, *A Natural History of the Senses*

"the black of the void"—Gary Shteyngart, *Russian Debutante's Handbook*

"a black eye ... in the richest inks of Tyrian [rare purple dye], chartreuse, and plum"—Donna Tartt, *The Secret History*

"blue as the sky in a Book of Hours"—John Banville, *The Untouchable*

"the bluest eyes ... like small drops of September sky" —Colum McCann, *Let the Great World Spin*

"a green-green-green that makes you want to cry" —Sandra Cisneros, *Caramelo*

"The green[,] ... a seemingly iridescent emerald that contained within it the essence of both light and water"—Anita Shreve, *The Last Time They Met* "the achingly fluorescent green"—Diane Ackerman, *A Natural History of the Senses*

"white as glacier milk"—Janet Fitch, *White Oleander*

"the yellow of all yellows, the yellow that every other yellow secretly wishes to be"—Redmond O'Hanlon, *Into the Heart of Borneo*

DELICIOUS

* Savory
* Refreshing
* Appetizing
* Virtues of Food or Drink
  (See also under: "Joy-Giving")

TASTIER THAN UNBELIEVABLE

In part, this book was prompted by a public television program critiquing Chicago-area restaurants. Each week the host assembled a fresh reviewing panel of ordinary diners. Well—not all of them ordinary. Illinois Senator Barack Obama was one of the earlier reviewers, though his expansive, articulate comments were not aired until they found their way to YouTube years later. But the other round-table critics were as ordinary as most people in how they reduced extraordinary dining experiences to three or four less-than-appetizing superlatives.

Dishes like pit-roasted thigh of antelope in sesame-thickened mustard sauce earned the juiceless adjective *unbelievable*. A napoleon of pumpkin mousse and spiced jasmine rice with a warm pear essence would top out at *amazing*. And waiters pirouetting through exotic settings as they sang opera, brandished flaming skewers, and delivered trios of aged Mediterranean ports garnered a ho-hum *awesome*. Week after week, panelists of all stripes failed to transcend these few terms, except for an occasional *fabulous* or *delicious*.

As I sat watching close-ups of *eye-mistingly exquisite* dishes, *provender for the gods*, and *nectareous* desserts, I was struck by the paucity of language we have at hand to acclaim one of the most pleasurable experiences on earth. I doubt that I, under the camera's eye, would have waxed any more eloquent; but I began thinking that a list of more celebratory terms might be useful to writers, critics, bloggers, and all who wish to lick their chops in words.

Wine lovers have already developed an appreciative language for the delights of the grape (see sidebar "Acclamatory Terms for Wine"), at the same time attempting a standardization of terms for specific qualities. But wine or any other drink or food can be acclaimed with more general terms, such as those I've suggested under "Great,"

"Joy-Giving," and even in rare cases, "Sublime." For example, a vegetarian burrito I consumed recently was a *miraculous alchemy* of simple ingredients into *perfection wrapped and bundled.*

Terms more targeted to food, however, can add texture or specificity to one's acclaim. I can't say that all the Indian dals and makhanis I enjoy are *eupeptic*, but they dance a *tarantella on the tongue* that lifts my soul.

I must advise here—as I might have done under any category—that while superlatives and other modifiers enable us to acclaim things quickly and forcefully, the most persuasive language is often the very names of the things—the particulars, especially sensual particulars like food. Good writers know that the particulars of a feast can be worth a dozen superlatives:

> "[P]latters of mutton croquettes, fish chops, onion pakoras, ghugni with puris, samosas, chutneys."
> —Bharati Mukherjee

> "[S]pitted lamb, prairie oysters, sweet corn, giant shrimp in Tyler's ketchup sauce, oven rolls, a keg of sour pickles, melons, ripe Oregon peaches made into deep-dish pies...."
> —Annie Proulx

Will you excuse me? I think I'm drooling.

TERMS

airy on the tongue
aged by nature
amalgam of flavors, an
ambrosial
amontillado, a draught of (*ref.*, rare sherry, fatally tempting in Poe tale)
amorously prepared
argument for carnivorism, an
amuse-bouche, an (*Fr.*: mouth-amusing bite-size appetizer from the chef)
artisanal (skillfully crafted)
Asian-inflected (—Sam Sifton)
autumn-smoky
bang delicious (very)
banquet-worthy
belly banquet, a
binge-worthy
bingey-pleasing (*AUSTRAL*, belly-pleasing)
bistro-light
black-tie vittles (fancy food)
bonanza for the belly, a

bone-delicious
bon-vivant fare (for lover of luxuries)
bordello for the taste buds, a
boutique dish, a
brazenly flavored
buttery
cachet of culinary genius, a (cachet = quality or official mark)
cannonade of flavors, a
carousel of flavors, a
case for the sense of taste, a
cheeky chew, a (playfully impudent)
chef's chef d'oeuvre, the (masterwork)
chin-drippingly juicy
clear-the-decks wave of flavor, a
comfort food for gourmets
comfort food for the gods
communion with Bacchus, a
communion with Annapurna, a (*ref.*, Hindu goddess of

harvest, food)
complexly layered
concerto of sweet and sour, a
conjuring of flavors, a
cordon bleu (prepared to a blue-
    ribbon standard)
cordon bleu, a (blue-ribbon chef)
creamy
crème brûlée, the (custard
    covered with hard baked
    sugar; top-off to a meal)
crisp/crispy
crunchy
culinary canon, of the (of the
    approved or sacred values or
    rules)
culinary classic, a
delicate
degustation to cherish, a (a
    careful, appreciative savoring
    experience)
degustatory rapture
delumptious
divine path to repleteness, the
    (satisfying fullness)
divine path to satiety, the
divinely edible
down-home
dream cuisine
earthy

Eden for the edacious (voracious
    eaters)
eminently scarfable
emperor's repast, an
enshrined in the pantheon of
    tastes
enthrallingly flavored/textured
enticing
epicurean (fit for sensual indul-
    gence)
eruption of flavor, an
eupeptic (good for digestion)
evocation of divine savor, an
exotic
exquisite, case closed
eye-mistingly exquisite
fearfully tasty
fissionably seasoned
fit for a sultan
flavor surge, a
"flavors as emphatic as a smack
    in the chops" (—R. W. Apple
    Jr., *Apple's America*, 2005)
fluffy
fluorescently aromatic (flower-
    like)
food-fiend's paradise, a
foodie heaven
force field on a plate, a
fragrant

free-range and oven-fresh
freshness defined
fruit glowing with earthlight
fusion made in heaven, a
garden party on a plate, a
gastronome's delight, a (connoisseur of food)
gastronomic garden party, a
gastronomically witty (—Sam Sifton)
gets a clean bill of taste
gift to the *kishkes*, a (*Yi.: kishkes* = guts)
glad tidings for the gullet
godly grub
goes down smooth
good to the last morsel
gourmand-goading (inducing hearty, excessive consumption)
gourmet (fine food)
gourmet gold (perfect for a connoisseur of fine food)
gulp-worthy
gustation made godly (act of tasting)
gustatory lagniappe, a (small or extra gift bestowed by tasting)
gustatory ravishment, a (pertaining to taste)
grubalicious

hallmark of foodocracy, a
hauntingly flavored
haute gastronomy
heady
heaven on a fork
heirloom/heritage (bred as fancy, nonhybrid cultivar; e.g., tomato)
heroic dose of seasonings, a
high tea for the taste buds
holy grail of food lovers, the
holy union of sweet, salt, and sour, a
honeycomb of sweet, a
honeysome
hunger-whetting
imperial dish, an
incendiary pleasure, an
inspired
inspissation of ecstasy, an (thickened liquid, as rich soup)
intensely flavored
inviting
jubilation of flavors, a
juicy
just gardened
just harvested
kishke-warming (*Yi.: kishske* = guts)
"kneebucklingly sweet"

(—David Foster Wallace)
lemony
light
like stolen sweets (tastier for being illicit)
loaves and fishes à la chef
locally raised, free-range, grass-fed, hormone-free, organic savor, a
love at first sniff
love between the teeth
luau, a (lavish Hawaiian feast, or like one)
Lucullan banquet, a (sumptuous, epicurean)
lunch as pure luxe (luxury)
lushly ripe
luscious
luxury on a plate
manna (divinely provided sustenance)
manna for the innards
manna for your mush (mouth)
manna out of mush (transformed to unexpected divine provision)
melts in the mind's mouth
meteor shower of spices, a
minimalist masterpiece, a
    (—Martha Bayne, *Chicago Reader*)
miracle in your maw, a
moist
mother lode of flavor, a
mother of all munchies, the
mother of all umami, the (deliciousness)
mouth-tingling
mouthwatering
must-eat, a
nectarous (sweet and delicious, like divine nectar)
news-flash fresh
noshalicious
not your meat and potatoes
nutty
olfactory orgy, an (*ref.*, sense of smell)
opulence in a spoon (lavish richness)
opulently garnished
out-and-out scrumptious
palatal bliss
palatal heaven
palatal love-in, a
palatal paradise
palatal wake-up call, a
palate party, a
palate-perfect
paradise on a plate

pedigreed palate, for the

peppery with a vengeance

perfection on a plate

pick-it-clean delicious

pièce de résistance, the (*Fr.*:
featured dish)

pie-chopper perfect (perfect for
the mouth)

pie-hole heaven

pie-hole perfection

pig-outably tempting

piquant

playfully blended/fused

plate-licking good

pleasantly sating

presto classic, a (very rapid)

provender for the gods

pungent

pure yumness

puts a crowhop in your craw (a
buck-jump in your stomach)

pyrotechnically spiced

quenchingly refreshing

rampantly spiced

redolence of Eden, a (scent)

redolent (aromatic)

regalement, a (entertainment by
sumptuous feast)

regaling (providing a sumptuous
feast)

resonant of ancient delights

rico!/rica! (*Sp.*: delicious)

ricochets from taste bud to taste
bud

robust

rustic

sacriluscious (forbidden but delicious; var. of *UD*'s "sacrili-
cious")

salivary

salvo of flavors, a

sapid (assertively, pleasantly
flavorful)

saporific (flavorful)

scrumdiddliumptious

scrummy (*UK*)

seal of good flavor, the

searingly spiced

seductive

shamelessly lickable

slap-up and savory (*UK*, well
provisioned and tasty)

slice of vegan/vegetarian heaven,
a

slurpworthy

smokin' and saucy

snug harbor for the hungry, a

soigné (*Fr.*: carefully prepared)

spring-fresh

steaming in its heavenly juices

sublime spread, a
sublimity on a spoon
succulent
suffused with flavor (spread through)
sultan's repast, a
sultry dish, a (warm, seductive)
summa cum yummy
summer-sweet
summery savor, a
"supernally buttery beef" (—Anya von Bremzen, *Food & Wine*)
"superstratum of ethereal crispiness," a (—Mike Sula, *Chicago Reader*)
supper cum laude (with highest praise)
supremely satiating
swashbuckling swallow, a
sweet mouth-memory, a
sweet ruffling of the taste buds, a
sweetest breath of yumness, the
sweetly fermented
swoon-per-spoon
Sybarite special, the (*ref.*, one devoted to luxury and sensual pleasure)
symphony of flavors, a
table d'hôte at the Dream Café (restaurant's fixed or featured dinner)
tamborito on the tongue, a (drum-driven Panamanian dance)
tangy
tantalizing
tantara on the tongue, a (fanfare)
tarantella on the tongue, a (whirling dance)
tart
taste fiesta, a
taste for all time, a
taste of paradise, a
tender
thermonuclear spice, a

"[O]n the tongue they put up a slight resistance before dissolving into a *tart* blast of honeyed squishiness that initiates dopamine overload."
—Mike Sula on Vietnamese lychee jelly cubes, *Chicago Reader*, June 10, 2010

three-stage palate-pleaser, a
three-star Michelin
thrilling ferment on the tongue, a
tongue-awakening
tongue-cooling
toothsome
top-grade belly-timber
toys for the mouth
trencherman-basic (*ref.*, big eater
off wooden platter)
true yum-osity
umami unfurled (*ref.*, the fifth
taste, deliciousness)
umami-grade (the fifth taste,
deliciousness)

verdict in: delectable!
"Viagra on a plate" (—Silvena
Rowe)
virtuous esculent, a (—Patrick
O'Brian: esculent = an edible))
vittles for voluptuaries
weapon of mass delectation, a
(enjoyment)
wedding feast, a
where delicious goes to dine
wholesome and hearty
yumtious
zesty

"A taste older than meat, older than wine. A taste as old
as cold water."
—Lawrence Durrell, *Prospero's Cell*, 1957

ACCLAMATORY TERMS FOR WINE

The brief definitions here draw from nuanced discussions found in *Winetaster's Secrets*, by Andrew Sharp, Warwick, 1995; redwinebuzz.com; "A Glossary of Wine Terms," on eRobertParker.com.; "Wine Lexicon," on wineloverspage. com; and other sources of wine terminology. Many of the terms can be applied to solid food as well as other beverages.

accessible (ready to drink and enjoy, sometimes earlier than expected)

aggressive (immediate, forward taste sensation)

aromatic (rich primary aroma)

backbone, good (full body, balance of tannins, fruit, acid)

balanced (harmony of taste, smell, feel)

big (ample tannins, acids, alcohol, etc., for intense feel)

brawny (full-bodied hefty, weighty)

bred, well (quality grape, soil, climate, etc.)

bright/brilliant (clear of suspended matter)

brooding (intense, with depths of complexity)

character, good (positive components, personality)

chewy (rich, heavy, fleshy mouthfeel)

clear (no suspended matter)

{CONTINUED}

clean (nothing "off" in odor or taste)

complex (multiple components making for good sniff and
taste)

consistent (elements appropriate to one another)

crisp (refreshingly drinkable firmness, no cloying acidity)

decadent (opulent fruit layers, huge bouquet, plump
texture)

delicate (pleasant medium-weight body, as in Pinot Noir)

deep (layers of aromas and flavors in harmony)

distinguished (exceptional character and quality)

elegant (subjective term for grace, character)

fat (silky feel from good alcohol, extract, and glycerin, as
in Rhônes)

finessed (varying positive meanings)

finish, good (enduring, post-swallow pleasantness and
balance)

firm (pleasing acid–tannin balance in the mouth)

flowery (floral to the sniff)

focused (precise scents and flavors clearly delineated)

forward (matured quickly, ready to drink)

fresh (lively and cleanly made)

fruity (fresh-grape smell and taste)

full-bodied (as in thick-textured dessert wines)

generous (easily delivers its flavor)

great (top quality in the glass)

grip, good (felicitous meeting of acid, tannins, and

  alcohol, as in ports)
harmony, good (see "balanced")
heady (exceptionally aggressive, forward aroma)
hedonistic (sheerly joyful, pleasure-giving, if obvious)
herbaceous (natural wine aromas suggestive of herbs)
intense (textured, complex, vibrant)
jammy (pleasantly fruity)
lively (fresh, exuberant, thirst-quenching)
length, good (long pleasant aftertaste, not too long)
luscious (fruity, approachable, balanced)
lush (velvety, soft, richly fruity)
mellow (soft, mature, as in red wines)
mouth-filling (chewy, fleshy in texture)
nervous (racy, lively acidity)
noble (truly superior)
nose, good (aromatic)
peaking (balance reached in best qualities of youth and
  maturity)
peppery (stimulating aroma, positive complexity, not too
  raw)
perfumey (refined, attractive scent)
pétillant (light bubbliness)
piquant (refreshingly fresh acidity plus sweetness plus
  body)
quaffable (goes down easy in hearty drinking, as Beau-
  jolais)

{CONTINUED}

{CONTINUED}

racy (lively from high acids)
rich (deep quality of components—flavor, sweetness, etc.)
ripe (peak of maturity)
robust (mature, rounded, balanced)
round (soft-in-mouth, mature balance)
savory (flavorful, interesting)
silky (smooth-textured weave of components)
smooth (soft texture)
soft (not harsh or rough in mouth)
sound (senses find no faults)
steely (firm acid level)
supple (vibrant but yielding, attractive texture)
unctuous (lush, soft, velvety, intense layers)
velvety (referring to texture)
viscous (density of fruit extract, thick)
zesty/zingy (acidic crispness)

"The dish [foie gras served at Jean Georges restaurant, New York City] ... activated every sense with which humans are equipped: ... rich and as smooth as butter, its *silky* texture contrasting with the caramelized sugar, which shattered like a pane of microscopically thin glass against the teeth and tongue...."

—John Colapinto, "Lunch with M.: Undercover with a Michelin Inspector," *New Yorker*, Nov. 23, 2009

VINTAGE GOLD

alimentarious (nourishing)
daintiful
fine-palated
friand (delicate)
gorgeable
gusts the gab (*SCOT*, pleases the mouth)
hungrifying
lickerous
neat
peckish (appetizing)
relishsome
tooth-tempting

TRENDY

- Popular
- Stylish
- High-Camp fabulous
- Fashionable
- Latest Thing
- The New Fabulous Thing

FABULOUS ON STILTS

Which comes first, the trendiness or the acclaim? In pop and fashion it's a dizzying cycle. Hype generates buzz; buzz draws attention; enough attention, and some hot commodity gives the subject *big props*, spurring broader acclaim, viral publicity, more hype—ultimately creating a hit, a trend, a star.

It's a cycle that works fast but has a house-of-cards fragility to it. Often more style than substance, a trendy item wins exposure, then overexposure, and finally—especially in a wired world—loses its two vital attractions: novelty and personal relevance.

But meanwhile, we can enjoy hailing our trendy favorites in language that is itself trendy, campy, and entertaining. *Pizzazzy. Bedazzy. Zizzy. Dicty. Soigné. Glammy. Bling-blinged. Outré.* Take just a few terms for "dressed stylishly": Honey, you are *dapped down, garmed up, trigged out, mockered up, prinked, duggy,* and *snappydap.*

While some trend-related superlatives fade like yesterday's chic, others dig in for the long haul, and none more tenaciously than the word *fabulous.* Originally meaning "legendary," "mythical," or "like a fable," it has enjoyed more than 500 years as a synonym for "exceptionally good," "delightful," "astonishing," and the like. English and American teens embraced it in the 1960s, along with the shortened *fab.* Some usage authorities disdained it as a vogue word, overworked by advertisers and "the modestly educated." But dictionaries have validated its expanded use, and here it is still—on the lips of everyone gaping at something new and glamorous.

Apparently *fabulous,* like *great,* is one of those words that people like to say, bray, hiss, and twist. It is a star of this category's list, along with established variations such as *fabbo*, *fabe*, *faboo*, and *farbulous*. I've had some fun with it myself, exploiting the adjective's amiable shift into a noun. Such a grammatical shift—a rhetorical device called "enallage"—enables one to form locutions like "*a fountainhead of fabulous*," or "Into the room walked *a whole lot of fabulous*." It gets campy, this enallage. At times it even verges on the snarky—as does much of our acclaim for things that walk the thin line between fame and shame, hit and miss, hot and not.

Finally, take care with terms like *bedizened*, *braw*, *chichi*, and *lahdee* (see definitions), or risk losing your standing in the Ancient and Honorable Order of Fab.

TERMS

à go-go
a la mode
a.k.a. amazing
ablaze
Academy Award shoo-in, an
acclaimed
accoutered for action (fitted out, equipped)
adulated
aflame
alias fabulous
all new and now
all Prada'd
all Versace'd
all Zegna'd (men's luxury fashions)
alpha talent, an
American-Idolish
armada of fabulous, an
Armani'd up
arrived
arriviste (nouveau riche)
aswarm with props (proper respect from fans)

audience-proof (cannot fail)
augurs fame and fabulosity (predicts likeliness of)
awash in adulation
awesome meets amazing
Bastille-storming revolutionary
beau monde, the (the beautiful people, high society)
bedizened and proud (dressed unabashedly in showy attire—sometimes gaudy)
bellwether, a (trend leader or indicator)
bespoke to the yolk (custom-tailored)
beyond gothic
bezazzy (pizzazzy)
big box office
big draw, a
big-timer, a
biker-chic
bis! bis! (a continental "encore!")
blast of fresh, a
blazing

bling-blinger, a (hip-hopper with status)

blisteringly hot

block-rockin' (sensational)

boffo/boffola (excellent/smash hit)

bohemian bespoke (—David Colman, *New York Times*: artily tailored)

bollynollygollywood! (*ref.*, rash of world film-center nick-names)

bon ton (elegant form or style; in tone with correct fashion)

boom (*CAN*, pleasing)

boulevardier, a (stylish frequenter of fashionable locales)

bound for the big time

boutique

box-office

bravo!

bravura (dazzlingly artistic— sometimes showy)

braw (finely dressed—sometimes excessively)

brilliant meets fabulous

Broadway

broke a leg (performed well)

buffed and burnished

butta!

buzz, the

buzz bomb, a

campy

cap-a-pie prinked (dressed up from head to toe)

caparisoned (decoratively clothed, like a classic warhorse)

cat pack, the (flush, fashionable, celebrity set)

caution: diva at work

celebrated

Celebrity City

celebrity-bound

charismatic (of magnetic person-ality)

Che-chic (*ref.*, revolutionary Che Guevara)

chic

chic unique

chichi (self-consciously stylish)

classy

cloaked in fabulous

clobbered up (dressed in quality clothes)

collar-to-cloak bespoke (custom-tailored)

comer, a

cool Muther John, a (hip, trendy boy)

cool, classic, and kosher

couture (of designer quality)

couture galore (*ref.*, high-fashion design and clothing)

cred (street credibility as stylish; acceptance)

criss (*UK, JAM*: stylish)

crit-hit, a (*UK*, critical success)

crowd fave, a

crowd-pleasing

crunking (wildly exciting)

cynosure of stage and screen, a (north star, leading star)

da ritz

dap (dapper)

dapped down (stylishly dressed)

dashy

dead fabuolus

debonair

dernier cri, the (*Fr.*, the latest word)

designer regnant, the (ruling designer)

dicty (high-class stylish)

dolled

done up

Dr. Fabulous

draped (fitted out with jewelry)

dressed to kill and ravage

duded

duded up

duggy (stylishly dressed or fitted out)

earns-the-love

ebullition of fabulous, an (gushing overflow)

encore performance, an

encore!

eruption of fabulous, an

fab

fabbo

fabe (*UK*, fabulous)

faboo

fabuloso/a

fabulous gift-wrapped

fabulous in flower

fabulous in full

fabulous in the flesh

fabulous on stilts

fabulous unfettered

fabulous, end of story

fame magnet, a

famed

fan fave, a

fanfare of fabuloso, a

fan-my-brow fabulous

fantabulous

fantasia of fashion, a

farbulous (*UK*, far-out + fabulous)

far-famed

fash (*AUSTRAL*, fashionable)

fash pack, the (fashion industry shakers and movers)

fashion queen/king regnant, the (ruling)

fashionista!

fashionista's fantasy, a

fashion-ninja strike, a

fave rave, a (favored artist)

flamboyant

fleshed-out fabulous

followed on everything (*ref.*, on Facebook, Twitter, etc.)

fountainhead of fabulous, the

Fraternal Order of Fabulous, the

frontliner, a

front-row-seater, a

frosted (*UK*, ornamented with jewels)

"[T]his young artist has appeared unexpectedly among us, like an astronomic manifestation, a brilliant phenomenon in the starry firmament, a bright, shining, wandering star."

—Sholem Aleichem (Rabinovitch), *Wandering Stars*, 2008 translation

---

festooned with bling (garlanded with jewelry)

find, a

finished to a high shine

fissionable

fitted (trendily dressed)

fitted out and rigged

five-encore

flagship of fabulous, the

funky-fresh (fashionable)

fusillade of fabulous, a

gallant, a (smart, showy dresser)

galleria of glam, a

garmed up (short for garmented)

g'd up (*rap*: dressed up gangsta style)

gilded in glamour

gildy (*UK*, fancy)

glammy (glamorous)

"glass of fashion and the mold of form," the (—Shakespeare, *Hamlet*, 3.1)

glitterati fixture, a (*ref.*, fashionable celebrity set)

glitterati, of the (fashionable celebrities)

glittering

Golden Globe-worthy

got flava (has a distinctive stylishness)

got street cred (has credibility on the streets)

Grammy shoo-in, a

grande dame, a

Grauman's-bound (*ref.*, Grauman's Chinese Theatre, Hollywood, site of celebrity handprints)

great gobs of fabulous

great meets fabulous

grosser, a (gross-profit-making entertainment enterprise)

Gucci'd up

Guevarista! (revolutionary Che Guevara-styled)

guilty of high style

hardly obscure

hardly unheard of

haute!

headline-grabber, a

headliner, a

heads-up, the (an alert to something new)

heart-seizingly it

high-maintenance highness, a

high-stepper, a

holler (stylish, pleasing)

Hollywoodish

hot copy (as in news copy)

hot dope, the (news)

hot/hott

hotness, the

hotter than Methodist hell

hot-ticket

iconic

idolized

igneous (fiery, once molten)

I've-fallen-and-I-can't-get-up fabulous

in

in like sin

in high orbit

in the torrid zone

incarnation of fabulous, the

incinerating

inimitable (beyond imitation)

instant classic, an

irradiated

It thing, the
jazzy
Jennifer Aniston 2.0
jeunesse dorée, the (*Fr.*: wealthy, fashionable young sophisticates)
killa
la rage
Lady Charisma (magnetic personality)
lahdee (*UK*, fashionable—sometimes pretentiously so)
large (famous)
latest bulletin, the
lava-hot
left-bank (*ref.*, Parisian Left Bank district: unconventionally stylish)
lick, the (*UK*, the hot thing)
limelighter, a
live
long on glam
love magnet, a
luminary, a
luminescent
mad glamorous
Madame Fabulous
Madame Tussauds of stars, a (*ref.*, famed wax museum of notables)

Madonna 2.0
magnifique
mantled in new
matinee-to-midnight idol, a
megastar, a
meld of hot and hotter, a
meteoric
Michael Jackson 2.0
mile beyond marvelous, a
military chic
mockered up (*AUSTRAL*, dressed up)
molten
motherland of fabulous, from the
movin'
Ms. Marvelous
muchness of campness, a
muchness of flair, a
mug of the month, the
natty
new look, the
new svelte, the
newly minted
news-flash fresh
news flash: fabulous!
next big name, the
next big ripple, the
next big spark in the powder barrel, the
next big trigger, the

next-gen
Nielsen-rating ready
nimbus of new and now, a
nobby (chic, stylish)
no-frills glamorous
nuclear-furnace hot
oil-on-the-fire sizzling
on a hoachy roll (*SCOT*, lucky
    streak)
on fire

paparazzi magnet, a
phunky (*UK*, fashionably funky,
    as music)
pillow-lipped pouty
pimped-up (flashy)
pitilessly hot
plugged in
pre-disheveled look, the (—Jon
    Caramanica, *New York Times*)
prima donna, a

"Magda's rocking a dope Ochun-colored bikini that her
girls helped her pick out so she could torture me."
    —Junot Díaz, "The Sun, the Moon, the Stars,"
    Drown, 1997

---

onslaught of star power, an
oozing with style
Oscar-bound
out-front
outré (outlandishly far-out,
    unconventional, bizarre)
outrider, an
paladin of style, a (champion,
    defender)
panache with wings (dash, flair)
panachey (having flair, dash)

prime-time ready
primped, prinked, and preened
prinked! (decked out)
props magnet, a (proper respect
    from fans)
propsworthy (worthy of proper
    respect from fans)
rad redux ("rad" or radical style
    revived)
rad-chic
Radical Nation

radioactive

rebel drag

rebel-approved

rebel-chic

red-carpet

red-carpet staple, a

renowned

revolutionary

rickety-raw (fashionable, good-looking)

rigged up and ragged out

rive gauche (*ref.*, la Rive Gauche, bohemian Left Bank district of Paris inspiring a 1960s style: stylish)

Rive Gauche (Yves St. Laurent fashion brand)

rocketborne toward fame

rockin' glad rags (dressed up)

rogue-son-of-privilege look, the (—Jon Caramanica, *New York Times*)

roiling hot

runway royalty (fashion-show runway)

runway-ready (fashion-show runway)

salvo of style, a

Saville Row (attire of upmarket quality)

scorching

searingly hot

seat-filler, a

Sultan of Suave, the

sellout performance, a

severely stylish

sheathed in fabulous

sheathed in style

sheech (chichi, self-consciously stylish)

shoo-in, a

show stealer, a

showstopping

silk-stocking (dressed upper-class)

Sir Fabulous

skinny, the (hot inside information)

skyrocketing up the charts

slathered in fabulous

slumadelic (*ref.*, music of rap group Outkast: funky, driven street style)

smart-set regular, a

Smithsonian of style, a

smokin' hot

snappydap (smartly dressed)

snaz, the (snazzily styled)

socko-boffo (hugely good, popular, successful)

soigné (*Fr.*: stylishly polished, groomed)

sophisticate, a

spanking

spendy-dressed (dressed in pricey clothing)

spendy-trendy (expensively stylish)

spif, the (spiffily, smartly dressed)

splashy

sporty

spruced

spuzzed up (primped)

SRO (standing room only)

standing-ovation getter, a

star in supernova, a (final, explosive brilliance)

star of stage and scream, a

starbright

stardom-bound

star-quality

steaming

stonking fabulous (*UK*)

stormer, a (*SCOT*, a popular hit)

streets ahead (*UK*, far in advance of, superior to, rivals)

streetwise

style on stilts

style queen/king regnant, the (ruling)

stylin' and profilin' (being fashionable, looking stylish)

stylishly impetuous (impulsive with attitude)

suave

suited and booted (*UK*)

superstar, a

surefire box office

svelte

swank

swellebrated

swellegant

that'll play the big time

thermonuclear

this just in

this-just-in trendy

thrilly

tilts toward the times

togged up (dressed up)

tonky (Par., *NZ*, fashionable)

tony/toney (upscale stylish)

too right!

top banana of the bunch, the

top billing

torrid

trendsetter with tenure, a

trendsetting

très with it

très Che (*ref.*, revolutionary Che

Guevara)
tricked out (dressed up)
trigged out (attired smartly,
	neatly)
trigged up (made trim and smart
	in appearance)
tucked and twilled
tumultuously cheered
tumultuously coiffed
turned-out
unlaced and out there
upstager, an
uptown (stylish, upscale)
videogenic
voice of a generation, the
walking library of style, a
walks on the wild side
wallopingly fresh

what-next, the
whiff of new-mown, a
white heat
white hot
Who's Who-er, a
with éclat (dazzling, sometimes
	showy effect)
wow, the
wow-it's-now
wreathed in fabulous
young-turk approved
zazzy (showy)
zeitgeisty (in the spirit of the
	times)
zhooshy (fixed up, styled in
	showy way, especially hair)
zizzy (showy, fancy)

VINTAGE GOLD
WHEN THE BEE'S KNEES
NEED REPLACEMENT

Once it caught on in the roaring 1920s, there was no stopping it: Wags and wits formed phrases to mean "the latest thing" by combining an animal's name with a body part or item of clothing. From *the bee's knees* to *the cat's pajamas*, the menagerie grew and has been growing to this day, albeit with a retro flavor. Goofy and even surreal combinations make for the most interesting and perhaps most revivable superlatives. Here's a dozen you might have heard from any Betty Boop of the Flapper Age or her Charleston-dancing Charlie:

the alligator's adenoids
the cat's cufflinks
the clam's garters
the eel's ankles
the elephant's eyebrows
the gnu's shoes
the monkey's instep
the pig's wings
the sardine's whiskers
the gnat's whistle
the caterpillar's kimono
the snake's toenails

COOL

* Hip
* With-It
* Interjections proclaiming coolness
  (See also under: "Wicked Cool")

WHEN WORLDS COOLIDE

Sometimes I imagine other civilizations watching us, observing our language, and borrowing the word *cool* to describe the myriad things that tickle their antennae. That's how adaptable and irresistible *cool* is, a 1,500-year-old term that means somewhat less than cold and, since about 1950, somewhat more than "hot."

As early as 1930, African Americans were acclaiming hot stuff as cool, but in the '50s the word acquired a nuance beyond the merely stylish and exciting. Among jazz musicians and finger-popping followers, it came to signify an understated soulfulness, a mellow quality calling for a restrained, discriminating style of acclaim. Lexicographers Harold Wentworth and Stuart Berg Flexner said it implied "intellectual, psychological, and/or spiritual excitement and satisfaction, negation of mere obvious, physical, sensual excitement."

To be cool was a special thing, earned like flight wings, unlike the facile *kull* or *way cool*. Cool people decreed what was cool, whether bop, beat poetry, or a tie so narrow it was almost invisible. But like other punchy utterances, the word caught fire and in the next decades became a colloquial term of general approbation. A secretary of state called foreign policy cool. Cornflakes, or dad wearing a dress, or the neighbor's house exploding were now cool, according to television spawn of Beavis and Butthead.

It was hardly the first time a superlative lost its specificity: *Grand* once meant preeminent; *swell*, a fashionable dresser. But rarely does a popular slang term go general and then hang on to its popularity for what might be—in *cool*'s case—indefinitely.

Even as universal and enduring a term as *cool*, however, needs its synonyms, if only for novelty of expression. And since novelty is brief, especially in the digisphere, trend-conscious acclaimers (including me) wait like chicks with open beaks for the next stylish or funky candidate.

For this category I've selected current synonyms, recent ones, plus some still-spry retro items. Of course, by the time you read this, current may be retro and retro current; so it goes. I've also intensified terms (including *cool*) in a number of ways and suggested various new phrase formations to trigger your own inventiveness.

As you go down the list, you may be as puzzled as I am by how certain words have earned their street cred. Single-syllable length seems to help (*dope*, *tight*, *phat*, *fly*, *def*, etc.), as does being introduced by a rap or teen-movie star (*fetch*). Clever shortenings (*leet* for elite) and touches of rebelliousness (*gangsta*, *ill*) count for something, though not as much as in our next category, "Wicked Cool." But meaning? It doesn't always figure. Don't try to make more of the superlative *book*, for example, than that a certain numerical texting code pops it up before the intended *cool*.

You can say *book* and I'll say *bangin'*. But I believe that those other civilizations out there, the ones eyeing us, still favor *cool*—perhaps even call us Planet Cool, our hotheadedness notwithstanding.

TERMS

active
all that
alpha pup, an (—*WS*, marketing term for coolest kid in school)
alvo
Ambassador of Cool, the
amped
audaciously cool
bangin'
beast/beastly
beyond rad
Blu-ray cool
blunt
bomb diggity
bomb, da
bonged
bonza
boogies down
book
boom (*CAN*)
boss
bubba! (as in "dude!")
Buddhistically cool
buff

bumpin'
burger
butter
buzzed
Camp Cool
cannonade of cool, a
capo di tutti cool (*I*.: boss of all)
card-carrying cool
casual
catch of the day
cheeky
cheese-on!
chill
chilled out
chilly most
chron
citizen of the coolocracy, a
clean
clued-in
cohabitates with cool
cold-cockingly cool
Commonweal of Cool, the
compact cool
compendium of cool, a

concentrated cool

convoy of coolness, a

coo

cookin'

cool as froze collards

Cool Breeze (form of address for cool person)

cool embodied

cool from clew to masthead (*ref.*, bottom tie of sail to top of mast)

cool in high-def

cool on a bender

cool to his/her chromosomes

cool to the core

cool to the marrow

cool up the smokeshaft

cool with a vengeance

cool with attitude

cool with wings

coola-boola

coolio

coolsville

copiously cool

Countess Cool

cracking

crisp

critical

Crown Prince of Cool, the

crucible of cool, a (where cool is tested)

crump

crunk/krunk

cwazy (var. of "crazy")

cyrogenically cool (extremely low temperature)

dece (short for "decent")

deep

def

deft

dialed

Doctor of Cool, a

dope

dopified (made dope)

down

downtown

drained!

drippin'

dude/girl is collected!, the

dude/girl is *ensemble!*, the (*Fr.*: together)

dude/girl is meshed-in!, the

dude/girl is mortised!, the (tightly joined together)

duggy (cooly dressed or fitted out)

École de Cool (school)

El Camino Cool (Cool Way)

encamped in cool

extra cool

fetch (*ref.*, from film *Mean Girls*: cool, fetching, trendy)

fierce

finger-popping cool

fire

flagship of cool, the

flash

flinty

flip

fly

freezing cool

Freon cool (*ref.*, refrigerant component)

fresh

fridge cool

frigorifically cool (producing cold)

from-here-to-the-back-of-beyond cool

frosty

funky cool

funneled

game

gangsta/gangster

gar (manly cool)

geared

gelid (exceedingly cold)

genial (*Sp.*: cool, excellent)

génial (*Fr.*: cool, excellent)

gets down

ghetto

gleaming

godly

Googleliciously cool

googolplex of cool, a

got burn

got her/his/its cool on

got street cred

got the patent on cool

hangin' in space

hard

heavy water

hecka cool

hefty

hella cool

hip to the haps (happenings)

hip to his/her hormones

hittin'

honed

hosed-down cool

hype

Hyperborean (*ref.*, mythical denizens of extreme north)

hyperkinetically cool

icing!

ill

incalculably cool

inherently cool

innately cool

jammin'

jelly
jelly tight
just!
justful
keel-over cool
kewl
kickin'
killer
king (*AUSTRAL*)
King Cool
knows how to roll
koshah
laid-back
languorously cool
leet (elite shortened)
live
Lord of Cool, the
lunar cool, a
lush
manifestly cool
massive
master/mistress of mellowosity, the
master/mistress of the cooliverse, the
mellow to the marrow
member of the coolarchy
meta-cool
mint
minty

money
monsta
monster
nang/proper nang (*UK*)
narcotic
nervous
nimble!
nonch (*Par.*, *UK*, nonchalant)
nonchalant
non-heinous
notch
off da hook
off the chain
on
on time
oozing cool
oudish (*UK*)
ownage! (as in "rules!")
parties down
phat 2 death
phatty
Platonic Form of cool, the (perfect abstract idea of)
plays the chill (is calm and cool)
polycool
prime
profusely cool
proper
proper lush (*UK*)
quintessentially cool

radical

slammin'

rapid

slick

"I think it looks cool, looks *tight*, those scars and everything."

—Wells Tower, "Wild America,"
Everything Ravaged, Everything Burned, 2009

---

raw

reddlessly cool

revved

ringside

rocks no ass (*Par.*, Guyana use of "no ass" meaning "extremely" after verbs)

rolls

royally cool

rude

rugged

ruley

savvy and saucy (—Shaun White)

scary cool

schway/shway

screams (cool and fast)

serious cool

shibby

sick/sic

sly

smokin'

so cool he's/she's evaporating

spiked

sprezzatura cool (*I.*: makes it look easy)

spunky

spunky cool

squeaky cool

standup

starkers cool (nakedly)

staunch

stoopid

straight-line cool

straight-up cool

street-smart

suave

superabundantly cool

superconductively cool

sweet
swift
take-charge cool
tang-gay!
tangy
thermal
thick
tight
togetha
totality of cool, a
tough
trick

unflippable
unlame
uptown
ur-cool (earliest, original cool)
valedictorian of cool, the
vato! (*Sp.*: as in "dude!")
wahey!
wavy
waxa/whacker (*UK*)
well
wet
wholly cool

"Them joints is *wet*!"

—"The Wire," 3rd season,
9th episode, 2004
(said of plasma televisions)

---

trippy
trop/trop bien (*Fr.*)
tuff
twitchin'
über cool (extremely)
ultra

wiggy
wily
wired
wix (*UK*)
zonal
zoned

VINTAGE GOLD

bitchin'
bonus
core
crazy
far out
gone
groovy
hep
key
mean
outta sight
right on
sent
slammin'
smoove
solid
stompin'
swingin'
torrible
wild

WICKED COOL

- Rebelliously Cool
- Unconventionally Cool
- Weirdly Cool
- Antisocially Cool
  (See also under: "Cool")

A LITTLE BAD

Years ago I had an acquaintance who delighted in preaching his rogue morality to infants as they lay in their cribs. "Bad is good," he would chant, leaning into the squinting faces. "Wrong is right. Foul is fine." Today some of those babies might be the homeboys and home-girls perpetuating a kind of anti-universe of acclaim: negative means positive; *nasty* is excellent.

In the world of slang acclaim, such reverse rhetoric is hardly new; *bad* was sometimes used to mean "tasty" in the 19th century, and soon after, "thrilling," "exciting," "marvelous," and the like. Lexicographers have explained the device as ultimate understatement; that is, pushing *not bad at all* to *bad* itself.

But let's not take all the badness out of contrary terms for "excellent." The way *bad* is sometimes used in acclaim—say, for a weapon, a boxer, a hulking vehicle— it clearly toes the dark side, implying menace or harm.

Most of us do want to be a little bad. In adolescence it is almost mandatory to access one's inner thug, vampire, whatever. Slang in this "Wicked Cool" category offers a naughty edge, a bit more rebellion than the terms suggested under "Cool." It is mainly, though not exclusively, a glossary for juvies, essential for street cred and schoolyard, campus, skateboarding, rapper, and other creds. For adults? Wicked cool is fun and most effective when voiced—and voiced with mock attitude and hip-hop gestures: "That is *filthy*, yo!" But would I use *nasty* in an essay praising the works of humankind? No. Maybe.

TERMS

abominable

acrid

aggro (radical, aggressive, manic cool)

all raw

angry

animal

atrocious

attitudinal/attitudinous

audacious

bad

bad to the bone

badass

baddest

base

bawla, a

bestial

bitchen twitchen

blade! (as in "dude!")

blatant (*UK*)

blunt

brash

brazen

broken

brutal

buggin'

burly (surfer term: intimidating)

cadaverously cool

chulo (*Sp.*)

coarse

cold

cold-blooded

"[H]e has ... a whole lot of Southern California surfer *baditude* to his credit."

—Janet Maslin of author Don Winslow, *New York Times*, July 8, 2010

"Meka is the *illest* man with a pen next to James Watts."

—James Watts,
comment on XXLMag.com, April 19, 2010

coxcomb! (as in "dude!")
cray cray
curt
dange (*CAN*, short for
    "dangerous"; pronounced as in
    "strange")
dangerous
dank
demon
depraved
deranged
dire
dirty
dirty cool
dooming
evil
feisty
fiendish
filth
filthy
flagrant
freakin' freaky cool
funky cool

G (gangsta)
gangsta
gnarly (dangerous, challenging
    cool)
got baditude
grim
grimy
hard
hardass
hellified
hellish
hellish cool
hoodoo
horror (*UK*)
ill
ill-ass
illest, the
kickass
kill
killer
lethal
lost
lunatic

lurid

mad

mean

messy

mordant (biting, caustic)

murky

narcotic

nasty

out-of-his/her-cage

pathological

peccant (sinning, morally faulty)

picked clean

poco loco

psycho

pungent

putrid

rake! (as in "dude!")

raw

rebel chic

renegade rider, a

Rorschach-certified weird (*ref.*, psychological test using inkblots)

rogue dog (homie)

rude

ruthless

savage

scandalous

shameful

sick/sic

sinful

sinister

sorry

spooky cool

spun

stompin'

stupid cool

swass

tart

terrible

toxic

ur-weird (original, earliest weird)

vicious

vile

voodoo

vulgar

way sick

FORCEFUL

* Tough
* Powerful
* Determined
* Intimidating
* Competitive
* Procreative
* Fast

RAW-KNUCKLED, THERMONUCLEAR ACCLAIM

One way to make our acclaim forceful—attention-getting and convincing—is to associate it with powerful forces. *Sinewy* bridges. *Incinerating* wit. A *fissionable* fastball. Why hitch your wagon to feeble praise when you can harness the power of muscle, nature, even the atom?

We admire force and we fear it, often simultaneously.

We cower before a forked-lightning thunderstorm, but acclaim it as *earth-shattering* or *cataclysmic*. Football fans cheer a *brutal* hit on a receiver while fearing for the player's spine. A jolting, disturbing work of art wins raves as *galvanic*.

Qualities such as aggressiveness and recklessness, unappealing in one context, are laudable in another. We honor *combat-hardened* soldiers of a *juggernaut-strength* army, as long as they're on our side. *Hell-for-leather* racing drivers are applauded. Mythological and comic-book superheroes must be *crippling*, *indomitable* mountains of brawn, *unquailing nimrods*. Even the most repellant notions of force can energize acclaim: an *eviscerating* blow to terrorism; a *mutilating* political satire.

Organisms may come to harm and even die by force; but what some call the "life force" drives them to function, grow, procreate, and think. The various names for this force—*ch'i*, *élan vital*, *vis vitae*, *the vital force*—suggest ways to acclaim the exceptional and mysterious energy of living things. "Mother was *vis vitae itself*, a presence that animated everyone around her." Even the life force of plants—to *pullulate* and be *jessant* and *fructuous*—lends metaphors to the language of acclaim.

Some of our human life force shows up as "drive"—determination, persistence, and competitiveness. These are classic values of capitalism, and to acclaim them, no concept seems too ferocious. *Smashmouth, tooth-and-nail, there-will-be-blood*, and *take-charge-and-chew-butt* competitiveness is what most stockholders like to see.

Competitors who chew their way to the top, along with those who otherwise arrive there, acquire certain power labels meaning "leader." Whether these are terms of praise or mockery depends mainly on how the leaders are regarded. High regard: "My son the *top dog*, the *macher*, the *mogul*, the *kahuna*." As society has it, most such terms are slanted toward men, a bias that is no prize when it comes to expressions of low regard: "How did that jerk get to be *head honcho*, the *nabob*, the *big cheese*, the *muckety-muck*?" And how did he? By *uncompromising*, *unremitting*, and *unsparing* tactics, *cutthroat* determination, and *pugnacious* persuasion. Or maybe his mother owned the business.

TERMS

abrading

adamantine (unyielding, diamond-hard)

adrenalined

alacritous (eager, speedy readiness)

all briskness and bristle

all pluck

all-powerful

all-subsuming (encompassing within)

almighty

amped/amped-up

anvil-forged

aquiline (eaglelike)

argument-ender, an

artillery-grade

at full sail

atom-smashing

Attila 2.0

authority, the

avalanchine

ayatollah, an

backbone, the

balls-out bold

bare-knuckled

"Him the Almighty Power / hurled headlong flaming from the ethereal sky / with hideous ruin and combustion down / to bottomless perdition: there to dwell / in *adamantine* chains and penal fire, ..."
—John Milton, *Paradise Lost*, 1674

anchored in granite

anchoring

battle-tested

beefed

bestial
big cheese, the
big dawg
big hitter, a
big Mach (*ref.*, Mach 1 = speed
   of sound)
Big Man, the (God)

body by Peterbilt (truck maker)
body-slammer, a
bone-crusher, a
boots-and-all committed
both-barrels blazing
bracing
brass-knuckles tough

"[C]ritics wrote of her ... galloping chords ... and her
broad dynamic range, from shadowlike pianissimo to
artillery-grade forte."
—Ben Fountain, "Fantasy for Eleven Fingers,"
Brief Encounters with Che Guevara, 2006

---

big potato, the
big-play guy/girl, a
bigfoot, a (dominating figure or
   medium)
bigwig, a
bionic
bionically buff
biting
black-belt bad
blistering
blood-bleaching
bloody but unbowed
blowtorch, a
blunt

brawny
breaded (wealthy)
breakneck (recklessly fast)
brisk
broncobuster, a
broncobusting tough
bruising
brutal
bulked (muscular)
bull-by-the-horns leader, a
bulldozing
bulwark, a
bust-head bad
bust-nose bad

buttressing

caffeinated

cannonball express, a

cannonball, a

caporegime, the (*I*.: second in
command, as a Mafia lieu-
tenant)

carapacial (shelled)

case-hardened

cast-iron

cataclysmic

catapulting

caudillo, a (*Sp*.: military head of
state; overlord, boss)

centripetal pull, a (drawing
toward the center)

charged

ch'i/chi/ki/qi in full flow (*ref.*, life
force, energy)

ch'i/chi/ki/qi-powered (*ref.*, life
force, energy)

ch'i/chi/ki/qi-raising (*ref.*, life
force, energy)

chews butt

clawing

closer, a

cock of the roost, the

cocked, locked, and rocked
(ready for battle)

cogent (forcefully convincing)

cold-cocking (knocking out)

collision-force

combat-hardened

combat-ready

combustive

comes out shooting

cometlike

compelling

concussive

connected

cosmic clangor, a

cower-before omnipotent

cranked

crescendo, a (increasing loudness
or force)

crippling

crunching

crusher, a

crusher, the (something powerfully decisive)

cutthroat competitive

cyclonic force, a

czar/tsar, the

decisive

deluge

diehard, a

dignitary, a

dogged

double-barreled

doughty (determined, brave)

draw-first-blood competitive
dreadnought, a (*ref.*, heavily
armed ship; fearless person)
drive-by trash-talker, a
drubbing
durable
dynamic
dynamo, a
earthmoving
earthshaking
earth-shattering
el que más mea (*Sp.*, Cuba:—
Arturo Arabitg: brave, tough;
literally "he who pees most")
élan vital itself (organism's
force of growth and adaptive
change)
electrodynamic
enforcer, an
eruptive

sion or abundance)
fast-laner, a
fearful tough
fecund (fruitful)
fertile
fertilizing
feverous (fevered, feverish)
fiercely determined/committed
fiery
finisher, a
fireball, a
firebrand, a (powerful agitator)
fire-breathing
fired-up
fire-eater, a
fissionable
flinty
flourishing
force of nature, a
force to contend with, a

"An *eviscerating* wind blew in from the canals."
—Elif Batuman, *The Possessed*, 2010

---

eviscerating
explosive
exuberant (increasing in profu-

forged
forged-steel
forked lightning (lightning that

branches into zigzags)

formidable

fortifying

fortissimo (loud)

fracturing

fructuous (productive, fruitful)

fueled up

full-throttle

fulminant (coming on suddenly, explosively)

fulminating (exploding)

gale-force

galvanic (jolting)

game

gate-splintering

gavel wielder, the

girding (readying for conflict or challenging activity)

gladiatorally aggressive

go-getter, a

good to go

got burn! (*ref.*, rocket engine burn)

got game (has winning, competitive skills)

"got some hard bark on him" (—Joel and Ethan Coen, film script, *No Country for Old Men*)

grandee, a

grinder, a

gritty

gut-buster, a

guts-up (extremely gutsy)

gutty

hairy-hearted

hammering

hand-to-hand competitor, a

happened (of an individual become successful)

hard

hardball

hard-boiled

hardened

hardbound

hardly a featherweight

hardy

has backbone

has heart

has the killer instinct

hatchet man/woman, a (specialist in firings or other cutbacks)

H-blast scary

headman, the

heart-blanching (removes color)

heavy hitter, a

heavy-duty

heavyweight

hegemonic (having influence over another state, region, group,

etc.)
he-hombre
hell-bent
heller, a
hell-for-leather determined (reckless, fast)
hench, a (strong muscular person)
Herculean
hickory-hard
hide of tigers, like a
high muckety-muck, the (important but often arrogant person)
high-energy particle, a
high-pressure
high-testosteroned
higher-up, a
highflier, a
high-stakes gambler, a
high-test
high-test estrogened
high-voltage
high-wattage
holds the big cards
hombrón, an (*Sp.*: big man, a stud)
honcho, the (someone in charge, sometimes self-importantly)
Hubble-eyed (*ref.*, the space telescope)

humbling
hummer, a (fast baseball pitch)
Hummer, a (*ref.*, brand of heavy passenger vehicle)
Hunnish
hurricane-force
hustlerati, the
hypersonic (at least five times the speed of sound)
ignescent (sparks when struck)
ignipotent (ruling fire; fiery)
illuminati, the (supposed secret masterminds)
immovable
impelling
imperiling
imposing
impregnable
incinerating
indomitable
inexorable (unalterable, unyielding)
intrepid
invincible
iron ass, an (tenacious person)
iron-fisted
ironman/woman
ironwood-hard
irrepressible
jacked

jarring
jessant (shooting up straight)
jet-force impetus, with
juggernaut-strength (crushing
   force)

landslide, a
Large-Hadron-Collider spin, a
   (*ref.*, world's largest particle
   accelerator)
leap of leopards, like a

"Freddie Altaminaro ... moved like a spirit raptured to
heaven.
                              —T. Coraghessan Boyle, "La Conchita,"
                                    Wild Child, Viking, 2010.

---

juiced
juiced-in (politically connected)
kahuna, a (powerfully wise
   person)
kickass
kick-ass tough
kill-the-whole-kingdom-and-
   phylum ferocious
kinetic
kingpin, the
knockout artist, a
KO/kayo king, the
Kundalini ascending (body's
   powerful, coiled energy rising,
   as in Yoga)
lacerating

leathernecked
leathery
leonine
life-force-driven
like kryptonite to Superman
   (debilitating)
long-ball hitter, a
"low-center-of-gravity guy, a"
   (—John Madden, others)
Mach 5 (five times the speed of
   sound)
macher, a (*Yi.*: big shot; important man)
macho (emphatically masculine)
made (of an individual elevated
   to power)

mad-fecund

magisterial

magnate, a

magnum force (*ref.*, high-explosive firearm cartridge)

mail-fisted

mana to spare (*ref.*, supernatural power in body: influence, authority)

mandarin, a (elite, high-ranking, powerful personage)

man-mountain, a

manned-up

mano-a-mano competitive (*Sp.*: hand-to-hand)

martial

master/mistress of the universe, a (able to make big moves, as in finance)

meat-eating

medieval (fierce, cruel)

megaton and a half, a (megaton = explosive force of one million metric tons of TNT)

meteoric

militant

mogul/mughal, a (important, powerful person)

mojo-powered

money baron, a

money mogul, a

monster-truckish

mop-the-floor-with-you scary

moxie itself (aggressive boldness, nervyness)

Mt. Anzac at Gallipoli, a (mountain insurmountable by Australian troops)

"muscle in his step" (—Colum McCann)

mutilating

nabob, a (powerful—as in wealthy—person)

naked steel

nerves of titanium

nimrod, a (mighty hunter, mighty man)

no tea party

nob, a (*UK*, a person of social distinction)

no-holds-barred competitive

no-quit trouper, a

not exactly powerless

nuclear

oak-hewn

oligarch, an (leader of small, powerful governing group)

out-the-blowhole attention-getting

overflowing

overhead smash, an (tennis shot)

overmastering

overwhelming

packing iron (*ref.*, carrying a gun)

panjandrum, a (an important person; used playfully and sometimes meaning inflated)

pants-wearing

paralyzing

paroxysmal (convulsive)

percolating

persevering

petrifying

pile-driving

pistoning

planetary momentum, a

plangent (loud, resounding, plaintive)

plenipotentiary (invested with full power of a position)

pneumatic

pollinating

potent

powder keg, a

power player, a

powered-up

powerhouse, a

prana (life-sustaining force, vital energy, Hinduism)

pressurized

primed for a killing (financial)

primum mobile, the (*L.*: the first moving; prime mover)

propelling

psyched

pugnaciously persuasive

puissant (powerful)

pullulating (germinating or breeding rabidly/abundantly)

pumped

punchy

puncture-proof

purpose-driven

puts your atoms in orbit

quail-before awesome

queen bee, the

quick-turn-burned (*ref.*, in-air jet refueling: recharged)

rabid

radiating

radioactive

raging

raise-the-moat fearsome

Rambo, a

rammish

ramjet-propulsive

rampageous

rampant

ramrod, a

raw
rawhide
raw-knuckled
redoubtable (fearsome;
   commanding respect)

scare-spitless tough
scorched-earth tactician, a
score-settling
scrambler, a
scrapper, a

"In his grave, Franklin Roosevelt is spinning like an atomic dreydl."

—Philip Roth, *Sabbath's Theater*, 1995

---

reinforced concrete
resilient
resounding
resurgent (able to rise again,
   revive)
reverberating
ripped (muscular)
riptide, a
roaring
rocketborne
rocketing
rupturing
rutty
sachem, a (Native American
   leader; political boss)
Samson 2.0
scalding

scrotum-shrinkingly scary
seismic (like an earthquake)
seminal force, the
she who must be obeyed
shofar blast, a (*ref.*, insistent
   battle/ritual horn in Jewish
   faith)
shogun, a (Japanese warlord)
shtarker, a (*Yi.*: a tough guy)
Siddhi-powered (able to execute
   supernatural mind/body acts,
   Hinduism/Buddhism)
sidewinder, a (powerful punch)
sinewy
singeing
skipper, the
smash-face

smashmouth

snake-eater, a (Special Forces soldier)

solar force

solid hickory

souped

sovereign

spark plug, a

spellbinder, a (powerful speaker)

spunky

squall, a (sudden, powerful windstorm, often wet)

stalwart

stampeding

staunch

steadfast

steel-toed

steely

stinging

stoked

stop-a-bullet hardass

stout

string-puller, a

strong-armer, a

sucker-punch specialist, a

sultan, a

supercharged

superluminal (faster than the speed of light)

supernova, a (powerful, brilliant last explosion of star)

supersonic

supreme

surging

sweeping

table-turner, a

take-charge-and-chew-butt serious

Tarzan 2.0

taurine (bull-like)

tectonic (*ref.*, massive shifting plates of earth's crust)

tempered (hardened)

tenacious

teraflop-fast (teraflop = 1 trillion math operations/second)

teravolt or two, a (teravolt = 1 million million volts)

thaumaturgic (able to work miracles or magic)

there-will-be-blood competitive

thermonuclear

three-fisted

thrustful

thundering/thunderous

to be reckoned with

tooth-and-nail tenacious

top banana, the (person in charge)

top dog, the (leading person)

tornadic
tornado-force
torqued
torrential
tough customer, a
tough-shelled
trample-underfoot intrepid
transmuting (changing one form
    to another)
tsunamic
tumultuous (crowd-level riotous,
    upheaving)
turbocharged
turbulent
turns on the heat
tussler, a
tycoon, a
typhonic
unblinking
unbowed
uncaged
uncompromising
uncontainable
uncontrollable
undergirding
underpinning
undertow, an
unfaltering
unfettered
unflagging

unflappable
unflinching
unleashed
unquailing
unquivering
unrelenting
unremitting
unshakable
unsparing
unstoppable
unswervingly driven
upthrusting
ursine (bearlike)
vigorous
vis vitae manifest (*L.*: life force)
vis viva manifest (*L.*: living
    force)
vital force, the
volatile
volcanic
vulcanized (strengthened as if by
    manufacturing process)
vuvuzelan (*ref.*, insistent raucous
    horns of South African soccer
    fans)
walking force field, a
walking power grid, a
walking power plant, a
walking warhead, a
warlord, a

warp speed (fictional highest, superluminal speed)
warrior, a
weapons-grade
weight-trained
well-fixed
well-heeled
well-knit
well-padded
whip-cracking
whitewater (violently foaming rapids)
whitewash, a (unscored-upon victory)
wildfire
will clean your clock (thrash)
Wonder Woman 2.0
wrath-of-God awesome
yangy (having hot, light, active force of yang vs. opposite yin)
you breezed!
you butchered!
you detonated!
you drubbed!
you meat-axed!
you scalped!
you squelched!
you throttled!
you trampled!
zero-tolerant taskmaster, a

VINTAGE GOLD

big brains, the
brass guts, a
bright-eyed and bushy-tailed
his/her nibs (person in authority, demanding)
huckaback (tough fabric)
lickety-split
mettled
one tough cuss
rip-roaring
ripsnorting
rock-ribbed
stiff-rumped
tough as old boots
toughian, a
viripotent

CHALLENGING BELIEF OR EXPRESSION

* Unbelievable
* Incredible
* Indescribable
* Mind-Boggling

TO BELIEVE OR NOT TO BELIEVE?

Every few acts, Shakespeare's immortal characters find their beliefs challenged, but never their powers of expression. Horatio, for example, beholding the ghost of Hamlet's father, tosses off no less a declamation than:

> Before my God, I might not this believe
> Without the sensible and true avouch
> Of mine own eyes.

And those of us who strut and fret upon the stage of modern life? When the scene turns paranormal, our normal response tends to be *unbelievable* or *incredible*.

The words have become habitual, imbedded in our neurons and probably our DNA. In the list following, I offer several hundred alternatives to these weary utterances, yet I doubt if I'll ever stop uttering them. Even when my corporeal self goes into nova and I transmigrate into a cosmic worm hole, I'll probably sputter, "*Incredible!*"

I can't stop myself from saying the words; but in writing I no longer call on them to describe or acclaim anything significant. They are exhausted, thinned to gossamer from overapplication. They have come to mean little more than "rather good," or "irritating" (as in an unbelievable tax hike).

If I were writing about, say, an extraterrestrial at my front door, I'd want to underscore the degree and nature of its unbelievability, or at least convey my excitement about it. I would intensify the usual adjectives, go over the top: *It was hold-everything unbelievable. An outtake from The Twilight Zone. To-the-back-of-beyond unreal.* I'd want to distinguish the event from special but not necessarily unbelievable phenomena—things like a *dreamlike* evening at the Ritz or a *surreal* feathered gown on a reality dance show.

Even in speech, I labor to use the occasional alternative if it doesn't sound too labored. Perhaps *uncanny* or something akin to *beggars belief* or *defies reality*, but more forceful. After all, there are so many ways to test or topple belief and its partners: reality, credibility, logic, and reason. A few examples from the list: *blindsides belief, lampoons belief, clobbers credibility, derails logic, annihilates all reason, hijacks reason.* It gets brutal, but we are upending stubborn convictions.

In challenges to beliefs, the believing mind (or brain) might also be knocked around. The most common assault: *boggles the mind* or *mind-boggling. Boggle* in the sense of "startle" or "overwhelm" is thought to derive from Scottish terms meaning "ghost" or "goblin." The etymology is apt but there are scores of fresh alternatives to the overworked *boggle,* among them *mind-fritzing, mind-blitzing,* and *both-barrels mind-blasting.* (Substitute *brain* for *mind* if you prefer.) As I write these very words, in fact, the New York Stock Exchange is suffering a 20-minute, thousand-point decline of *brain-bludgeoning* unbelievability, as defenestrating investors might acclaim it on their way down.

TERMS

all agogging
all-bets-off unbelievable
annihilates all reason
annuls reason
apparitional
as _if_
assaults belief/reason
astonishing
atomizes reason
aurora of unreality, an
banishes reason
bankrupts belief
beanballs belief
beggars belief/expression
begrudges belief
beheads belief
belief-battering
belief-buffeting
belief-twitting
belies reason
belies the apparent
belittles belief
bereft of words, one is
beseeches belief

bewildering
beyond boggling
beyond fanciful
beyond imaginary
beyond language
beyond nomenclature
beyond _Ultima Thule_ (_L._: _ref._,
     farthest point reachable)
beyond utterance
bizarre
blackballs reason
blindsides belief
blitzes reality
body-checks belief
body-slams belief
bollixing (confusing)
bonce-banger, a (_UK_, bonce =
     head)
bonks the mind
both-barrels mind-blasting
bounces your brain on the ceiling
brain-addling
brain-bludgeoning
brain-boffing

brain-bollixing
brain-buggering
brain-curdling
brain-on-a-bender bizarre
brain-pulverizing
brain-rupturingly unreal
brain-scrambling
brain-spinning
brain-straining
brain-throttling
breaches logic
breaches reality
bucks belief
bucks credibility
buggers belief
bumfoozling
burdens belief/expression
busts belief's bullocks
butts up against reason
certified unreal
chew's reality's butt
chimerical (perceived, but
    improbable in reality)
circumvents reason
clear-the-decks, batten-down-
    the-hatches brain-blowing
cleaves credibility
clobbers credibility
cold-cocking (knocking out)
contra-credible

contra-cognitive
court-martials your convictions
crazy unreal
credibility-gapping
crushes reality
damns logic
decapitates reason
defenestrates all premises
    (throws out the window)
defies belief
defies credence
defies expression
defies perception
defies speech
deflates reason
demolishes perception
denounces logic
derails logic
derides reason
disassembles reality
disgorges conviction
disorienting
divorced from reality
dreamlike
dumbfounding
drubs reality
estranged from reality
eviscerates reason
expels belief/reason
explodes all precepts

fable, not fact, a
fantasyland
fingers reality
flabbergasting
flat-out unbelievable
flattens belief
flays credibility
fleeces logic
flooey-making
flooring
flouts reason
foils reason
furloughs reality
gear-grindingly illogical
gives reality the Bronx cheer
   (mocking, sputtering mouth
   noise)

grinds the gears of ratiocination
   (process of reasoning)
hallucinatory
head-bangingly unreal
hello, the impossible
hijacks reason
hold-everything unbelievable
hoovers away words (vacuums)
horsewhips reason
illusory
impales logic
implores belief
in a manner of speaking,
   unbloodybelievable
incarnation of amazing, the
incomprehensible
incredible uncaged, the

"[T]he temperature rose into the forties, and suddenly the air was charged with an *ineffable* sweetness, a perfume as of invisible flowers."
   —E. Annie Proulx, *Accordion Crimes*, 1996

---

gives reason the raspberry
   (mocking mouth noise)
gobsmacking (rendering speech-
   less)

ineffable (inexpressible)
inenarrable (indescribable)
inexpressible
invalidates words

"Their [the Human Eye Band's] second full-length release continues their musical mission with more *mind-derailing* time changes, ... hallucinatory overdriven echoplex, and a generally brutal assemblage of disparate elements.... By the second or third listen, you'll (hopefully) be too disoriented to think, analyze, etc."

—Matthew Smith,
www.hookorcrook.com, May 18, 2010

jams the brain
jettison-all-reason incredible
kayos cognition
kicks belief in the butt
kicks credibility in the crotch
kicks reality in the rear
knocks logic for a loop
knocks reality off its pins
lampoons belief
liquidates reality
logic meltdown, a
Magic-Kingdom unreal
mauls reality
maybe in an alternate reality
maybe in another dimension
maybe in the anti-universe
migraine-making
mind-bending
mind-blitzing
Mind-Boggling Boulevard

mind-bonking
mind-cleaving
mind-clobbering
mind-crumping
mind-cudgeling
mind-derailing
mind-diddling
mind-disintegrating
mind-dismantling
mind-fracturing
mind-frazzling
mind-fritzing
mind-gobbling
mind-gutting
mind-hemorrhaging
mind-incinerating
mind-jarring
mind-joggling
mind-macerating (softening by soaking)

mind-maiming
mind-mangling
mind-marmalizing (thrashing
    into marmalade)
mind-mashing
mind-mugging
mind-mushing
mind-mutilating
mind-muzzling
mind-pummeling
mind-razing
mind-riddling
mind-shattering
mind-splitting
mind-stopping

mocks credibility
mocks the apparent
moons logic
mouth-stopping
mugs belief
muting
never-neverish
nimbus of unreal, a (cloudlike
    aura)
nimiety of unreal, a (overflowing
    excess)
nonplussing (confusing)
nubilation of unreal, a (cloud
    formation)
off the map

"... I have nothing to say. It is a question we can only stare at in silence, like a bird before a snake, hoping it will not swallow us."

—J. M. Coetzee, *Foe*, 1986

---

mind-thwacking
mind-truncheoning
mind-vaporizing
mind-walloping
mind-zapping
mirage, a

off the reality grid
Og, Gog, and Magog brain-
    boggling
ontologically out there (beyond
    or at the fringes of theories of
    existence)

out of human range
out-of-body unreal
outtake from *The Twilight Zone*,
    an
otherworldly
overmuch
overthrows reality
overwhelming
Oz-unreal
pauperizes reason
pauperizes language/words
phantasmagoric (illusory, as in
    shifting, dreamlike illusions)
phantasmal
pillages belief
pillories belief (locks up for
    ridicule)
pinch-yourself unreal
pistol-whips reason
prostrates belief/certainty
    (throws flat to the ground)
pummels understanding
punctures logic
quarantines logic
rakes belief over the coals
reality belly-up
reality fading out now!
reality on a fast
reality on a toot
reality on recess

reality-rending
redonkulous
renders words useless
rift in reality, a
rules out perception
sabotages belief
salt my hide if I'm seeing this
sanctions disbelief
sandbags logic
saps belief
science-fictional
scorns logic
scorns reality
scuttles belief
sends reality packing
sheer astonishment, a
shoots logic in the foot
shreds belief to the bone
skewers words/expression
skews reality
skull-spinning
slaughters belief
so unreal it's illusory
so unreal it's null and nonexis-
    tent
so unreal it's unactual
sound-the-alarm unreal
spectral
speech-shattering
speech-stopping

splinters credibility
spoofs reason
spurns reality
squashes belief
staggers belief
stares down reality
startling
stills the voice
strains expression
stymies speech

trammels logic (shackles, restrains)
tramples logical thought
transmundane (beyond this world)
trashes reality
trim-sail-and-batten-the-hatches mind-blowing
turbulence of unreality, a
tweaks reason's nose

"Words, with their weight, have a tendency to fall like birds of prey on delicate ideas, carrying them away before they have a chance to reach fruition."
—Lyall Watson, *Lifetide*, 1979

---

stymies the senses
subpoenas belief
surreal
swindles reality
taunts belief
taxes credibility
tears the cover off logic
tests the senses
tips the scales of credibility
tongue-bindingly indescribable
tongue-stilling
to-the-back-of-beyond unreal

Twilight-Zone unreal
twits belief
uncanny
undercuts reality
undermines all credos (statements of belief)
ungluing
unreportable
unrool (*AUSTRAL*, unreal)
untenable (cannot be defended or maintained)
unutterable

unzips reality
uproots all faith
validates disbelief
validates doubt
vertiginously boggling (dizzy-
    ingly)
vetoes reason
voids reality
walks-on-water incredible
wig-walloping
will blow your circuit board
will blow your circuitry

will blow your mainframe
will crash your hard drive
will-o'-the-wisp, a (elusive glow,
    or anything that misleads one
    on)
wilts belief
withers credibility
words betray me
words collapse
words desert me
words forsake me
zeroes out belief

VINTAGE GOLD
YOU ARE KIDDING ME!

One of our most habitual belief-challenging outcries is "You have got to be kidding!" It makes the point; but demonstrative doubters will find many of our suggestions also suitable for exclamation, while a few vintage ejaculations (below) are worth mentioning for their color or vitality. Some oldies endure through association with a popular figure. John McEnroe's patented challenge to tennis umpires, "You cannot be serious!" became his acclamatory cry decades later in auto-rental commercials.

Come off it!
Did you ever!
Go on!
Heavens to Betsy!
In a pig's eye!
Like fun!
My foot!
No kiddin'!
Tell it to the marines!
Tell me another!
That cock won't fight!
Well, shut my mouth!
Your Aunt Mitty!

APPENDICES

APPENDIX 1

PREVIOUSLY OWNED BUT STILL RUNNING: 100 SELECTED ACCLAMATORY TERMS FROM RECENT CRITICISM AND ADVERTISING

Writers under pressure can't always pause to find novel superlatives. Nor does every situation demand originality. Sometimes a term in popular use—still energetic if not distinctive—is good enough for a job of praise or acclaim.

Below, I've pulled some 100 choice acclamatory words and phrases (including "blurbs") appearing in recent mainstream ads and critical writing, primarily in entertainment and the arts. A number of the most reliable "used" terms have earned a place in our main list as well.

alluring
arrestingly articulate
astonishing
astounding
bitingly funny
buoyant
breathtaking
captivating
certifiably hilarious
classy
combustible
compelling
corker, a
dazzling
delectable
devilishly entertaining
dizzying
earth-shattering
enormously compelling
exhilarating
explosive
extravagantly funny
exuberantly entertaining
eye-popping
first-rate
gloriously realized
grade A
gripping
groundbreaking
gusher, a

gut-wrenching
haunting
heart-stopping
heart-thumping
heartfelt
high-octane
hot-blooded
in-your-face hysterical
ingenious
instant classic, an
intense
irresistible
jaw-dropping
kick-ass
luminous
lush
magical
magnificent
marvelously bizarre
masterful
masterpiece, a
mesmerizing
nerve-frying
nimble
passionately spontaneous
phenomenal
pitch-perfect
poignant
provocative
pulse-pounding

radiant
rapturous
real deal, the
remarkable
revelation, a
ridiculously great
riveting
robustly entertaining
searing
seductive
sensational
shamelessly entertaining
sheer joie-de-vivre
simmering
sizzler, a
soaringly beautiful
sophisticated
stunningly gorgeous
stylish
sublimely spectacular
swooooon
ten, a
thought-provoking
thrillingly hypnotic
to die for
total knockout, a
touching
transcendent
transporting
triumph, a

two thumbs up
unforgettable
unsettling
vibrant
virtuoso
visceral
visually pulsating
white-knuckle
wickedly thrilling
wondrous

APPENDIX 2
50 WAYS TO TXT ACCLAIM

OMG, DATS SO NT GR8!

Only a small number of text-messaging or tweeting abbreviations stand for terms of praise. If texters want to go beyond the established code in their acclaim, they have to resort to words—but words ruled more by principles of shorthand than of grace. Still, words can mitigate the insults and obscenities that seem to dominate the typical texting glossary, which the unknowing could mistake for some kind of juvenile gang code.

But who's judging? Here I simply gather text code having to do with praise, enough for a working vocabulary. Though drawn from several established lists, the entries are not exhaustive nor are they elegant alternatives to *great*, *awesome*, and the like—just different means of representing those words. Texting code naturally sticks to most common terms and phrases of the vernacular; otherwise, it would become as onerous as foreign-language study. But even within stingy character-and-megabyte limits, you the gracious texter can mix code with more expressive language, 4 UR2 *amicable*, 2 *sapient*, nt 2 do so, RU nt?

1drfl ⇨ wonderful
2G2B4G ⇨ too good to be forgotten
2G2BT ⇨ too good to be true
5FS ⇨ five-finger salute
6Y ⇨ sexy
ADIP ⇨ another day in paradise
BAG ⇨ busting a gut
BBW ⇨ big beautiful woman
book/c%l ⇨ cool
CAAC ⇨ cool as a cucumber
CSA ⇨ cool sweet awesome
D&M ⇨ deep and meaningful
G1 ⇨ good one
G9 ⇨ genius
GLB ⇨ good-looking boy
GR8 ⇨ great
GUD ⇨ good
HNL ⇨ whole 'nother level
KAPBL ⇨ capable
LIBBY ⇨ life is better because of you
mazin ⇨ amazing
mjr ⇨ major
MKOP ⇨ my kind of place
MML ⇨ made me laugh
N1 ⇨ nice one
NcreDbl ⇨ incredible
NLL ⇨ nice little lady
OTT ⇨ over the top

PFT ⇨ pretty freaking (or f-word) tight
phat ⇨ pretty hot and tempting
QT ⇨ cutie
RL ⇨ real life
RNTUAQT ⇨ aren't you a cutie
ROTFL ⇨ rolling on the floor laughing
RW ⇨ real world
SLAW ⇨ sounds like a winner
TISL ⇨ this is so cool
TSOB ⇨ tough S.O.B.
UR2K ⇨ you are too kind
URH ⇨ you are hot
URTM ⇨ you are the man
VFM ⇨ value for money
VGC ⇨ very good condition
VN ⇨ very nice
WD ⇨ well done
wkewl ⇨ way cool
WOA ⇨ work of art
X-I-10 ⇨ exciting
XLNT ⇨ excellent
YAVIS ⇨ young, attractive, verbal, intelligent, and successful

APPENDIX 3

AN ALPHABET OF EPONYMOUS ACCLAIM

What sort of *Mickey Mouse* leads to a *Midas touch*? We can't say, but we can tell you that such name-based terms are called "eponymous." Names of real or fictional people underlie the eponymous names given to things and places. Simón Bolívar is the eponym of the eponymous "Bolivia"; Amelia Jenks Bloomer of "bloomers"; innkeeper Cesar Ritz of "Puttin' on the Ritz."

Many eponyms form not just nouns, but also adjectives—Bolivian, Christian, ritzy, etc. (See "Form Your Own," below.) Some can be stretched into adverbs, as in "He *Kafkaesquely* became a cockroach."

When it comes to praise and acclaim, eponymous modifiers bestow qualities of the admired eponym—the person—upon the modified thing. Call politicians *Lincolnesque* and they grow a heroic foot taller. The following alphabet of eponymous adjectives, with sample uses, suggests the range of possibilities for the device.

Austenian—after Jane Austen, English novelist.
Nora's romantic novels enjoy an *Austenian* popularity.

Byronic—George Gordon Byron (Lord Byron), English poet.
The *Byronic* beauty of his works overshadows his recklessness.

Confucianist—Confucius (Kong Qiu), Chinese thinker and humanist.
A *Confucianist* wisdom emerges from the poem.

Dickensian—Charles Dickens, English novelist.
She shows a *Dickensian* eye for character.

Emersonian—Ralph Waldo Emerson, American writer and philosopher.
Their all-embracing, *Emersonian* spirituality attracted followers.

Felliniesque or Fellinian—Federico Fellini, Italian film director.
Was it a lavish dream or a *Felliniesque* spectacle unfolding before us?

Gandhian—Mohandas Karamchand (Mahatma) Gandhi, Indian political and spiritual leader.
They succeeded by virtue of *Gandhian* courage and humility.

Hellmanesque—Lillian Florence Hellman, American playwright.
Her pursuit of justice was *Hellmanesque* in its intensity.

Iacoccian—Lido Anthony (Lee) Iacocca, American auto executive and business leader.
It would take *Iacoccian* guts and know-how to fix this mess.

Jordanesque—Michael Jeffrey Jordan, iconic American basketball star.
His *Jordanesque* grace distinguished him from the playground hustlers.

Kennedyesque—John Fitzgerald (Jack) Kennedy, American president, or Edward Moore (Ted) Kennedy, American senator and political leader, or the Kennedy political family in general.
They aspired to a *Kennedyesque* caliber of leadership.

Linnaean—Carl (Carolus) Linneaus, Swedish botanist and zoologist, father of modern taxonomy.
She had a *Linnaean* genius for naming and classifying her boyfriends.

Miltonic or Miltonian—John Milton, English poet and polemical essayist, author of *Paradise Lost.*
Who knew he could produce a work of *Miltonic* beauty and magnitude?

Napoleonic—Napoléon Bonaparte, French emperor and military figure.
He swept through Wall Street with *Napoleonic* drive and ambition.

Orwellian—George Orwell, pseudonym for Eric Arthur Blair, English novelist and journalist.
It called for an *Orwellian* grasp of truth behind the party's lies.

Pythonic or Pythonesque—Monty Python, an invented name in "Monty Python's Flying Circus," British television comedy show.
It wasn't just wacky funny; it was *Pythonically* funny!

Quintilianesque—Marcus Fabius Quintilianus, Roman educator, author of 12-book *Institutio oratorio*, a classic in educational theory and literary criticism.

Quintilianesque in breadth and insight, the paper astonished the jurors.

Ruthian—George Herman (Babe) Ruth Jr., iconic baseball slugger.

He took a *Ruthian* swing at the alien and cracked its carapace.

Solomonic—Solomon, legendarily wise king of ancient Israel.

The kid is four years old and already she's *Solomonic*.

Thoreauvian—Henry David Thoreau, American writer, naturalist, social critic, author of *Walden* and *Civil Disobedience*.

Seeking roommate with *Thoreauvian* passion for nature.

Updikeian—John Hoyer Updike, American writer revered for pitch-perfect language and storytelling.

You need an *Updikeian* ear to convey its sadness.

Vonnegutian—Kurt Vonnegut Jr., American author whose satirical brilliance manifested itself in science fiction novels and other works.

With *Vonnegutian* wit, she helps us endure a world gone mad.

Whitmanesque—Walt Whitman, American poet, essayist, and humanist.

He does everything with a *Whitmanesque* appetite for life.

Xerxesian—Xerxes the Great (Xerxes I of Persia), powerful ruler and conqueror.

Benny put a *Xerxesian* move on rival gangs.

Yeagerian—Charles Elwood (Chuck) Yeager, pioneering American pilot of supersonic craft.

She showed *Yeagerian* nerves biking through Manhattan.

Zorroesque—Zorro (Don Diego de la Vega), fictional, masked, Robin Hood-ish outlaw.

With *Zorroesque* flair, she took over the charity and doubled its giving.

"[*Avatar* is] an *Emersonian* exploration of the invisible world of the spirit filled with *Cameronian* [after director James Cameron] rock 'em, sock 'em."

—Manohla Dargis, *New York Times*

FORM YOUR OWN

Eponymous words offer unlimited alternatives to conventional terms of praise, although, as with all rhetorical devices, they should be used sparingly and aptly.

Start with a name recognized by your audience and having the desired positive associations. The best would-be eponyms are usually names recognized by a single word, rather than first and last name. An eponym based on a very common name should evoke a particular person, as with Jordan and Whitman in the sample alphabet. When too many people come to mind, the reference needs to be made clear with context: "There was a Kingian dignity to the sermon and the march that followed." Otherwise, the somewhat awkward form "Martin Luther Kingian" might be used, or "Martin-Luther-King-like" (the latter no longer an eponymous term, but a comparative simile).

What kind of ending does one add to a name? Should it be *-an*, *-ian*, *-sque*, *-ic*, *-ish*, *-al*, or some other? Standard dictionaries provide the endings for the most common eponymous adjectives, based on usage, but rules are scarce for new coinages. Pronunciation (keeping the original sound of the name), purpose, clarity, and formality are factors: *Whitmanesque* might sound better than *Whitmanian*. A *Plotnikian* theory, but a *Plotnikesque* dance move. *Jordanesque* because *Jordanian* can mean a person from Jordan. *Daffy Duckian* studies, but *Daffy Duckish* capers.

Keeping these factors in mind, start with the following guidelines, but check a standard dictionary for certain exceptions (e.g., Shaw becomes *Shavian*) and formations using particular classical and non-Western names.

FOR NAMES ENDING IN A CONSONANT

Add -*ian* (*Clintonian*). For flair, playfulness, better sound, or in art-related contexts, -*esque* might be used (*Daliesque*); it may also be more apt in modifying dynamic actions (a *Tysonesque* uppercut).

FOR NAMES ENDING IN E OR I

Add -*an* (*Gorean, Gottian*).

FOR NAMES ENDING IN A, O, OR Y

Add -*n*, -*nian*, -*esque*, -*ist*, or -*nic* to the name (or its root, dropping the last vowel) depending on convention, ease of pronunciation, and appropriate tone (*Maddonian, Lady Gagan, Presleyan, Neronian, Junoesque, Maoist, Platonic*). Names ending in *u* might need an added *v* before the adjectival ending (*Thoreauvian*).

In its brief notes on name-derived adjectives, *The Chicago Manual of Style* advises against forming eponymous terms from names that "do not lend themselves to such coinages." But where's the fun in that? A *Williamsesque* tennis player or *Snoop Doggian* rapper merits the coin.

APPENDIX 4

ALL-OUT APPLAUSE FOR
ACCLAMATORY ALLITERATIONS

Users of this book will find that many of my suggested, multi-word terms are alliterative; that is, they contain repeated sounds, as in *flat-out phenomenal*, *blues-banishing*, and *paradise on a plate*.

Easy to achieve and therefore prone to overuse, alliteration often gets a bad rap, depending on context. But before I'm charged with unseemly affection for the device, I plead that it functions honorably as an intensifying element of acclaim. Limited to appropriate targets of praise and two or three repeated sounds within a term, alliteration can put an innocent hop and skip in a superlative.

Akin to rhyme but pertaining to neighboring words, alliteration has three variations: repeated initial consonant sounds (labor of love); other repeated consonant sounds (pitch and catch) and repeated vowel sounds (blood and thunder). Some familiar samples illustrate both its variety and pervasiveness in our culture:

fan the flames
beans means Heinz
just do it
nattering nabobs of negativism
pig in a poke
mountain out of a molehill
neither rhyme nor reason
GI Joe
seventh heaven
cold shoulder
make or break
double-deuce juice (rap slang)

Though alliteration is a natural element in the development of language, it draws critical disdain in such contexts as bombast or barmy verse—or wherever it strains for effect. Nevertheless, the device enjoys a noble place in acclamatory language. Acclaim loves alliteration not only for its musical and rhythmical aspects, but as a mnemonic device—one that helps people remember the acclaim.

As Mark Antony honors the slain Caesar (in Shakespeare's *Julius Caesar*), such alliterations as "sterner stuff," and "kingly crown" stick to the ribs.

When stadium crowds praise America by singing its

national anthem, they tend to mumble their way through forgotten phrases, but they belt out the alliterative ones: "twilight's last gleaming ... rockets' red glare, bombs bursting in air ... oh say, does that star-spangled banner still wave ..."

Alliteration may be cautiously restrained in contemporary poetry and prose, but it stands tall in much of the writing we cherish, be it Dickens's "a long lamenting wail" or Coleridge's "In Xanadu did Kubla Khan / A stately pleasure-dome decree: ..." (—"Kubla Khan")

Before including an alliterative term among my suggestions, I have usually tried to imagine at least one appropriate context for it. Certain food marketers, for example, should not be put off by *perfection pickled and preserved*, even if love poets might find it cringey. All of which is a way of saying, in defense of the often-panned device:

If the alliteration fits, you must acquit.

APPENDIX 5
QUICK HABIT-BREAKERS: A STARTER SET

In the act of writing, one can choose patiently, even meticulously, from the thousands of suggestions offered in this book, developing a potent vocabulary of praise over time. But there's little chance to pore through a lexicon during conversation or digital messaging. New terms must come to mind even as old ones cling to the tongue like limpets.

Still, even hurried communicators can break free of worn superlatives. All that's needed is a starter set of alternatives, a modest number of terms likely to engage one's audiences. Such terms can be plucked in advance from the full lists; or, one can choose from the sample starters below, some 200 suggestions drawn from five main categories and offered in the way of encouragement.

Using new and unexpected terms may seem risky. It will often feel unnatural. But to play it safe in language is to make white noise. Once old habits are broken and the tongue adapts to those first strangers, one welcomes the opportunity to hail favorite things in fresh and persuasive ways—to have fun doing so. Users of any term should, of course, be aware of nuance, unless they can come up laughing from the occasional pratfall. (The main lists provide brief definitions of unfamiliar terms.)

For: great, amazing, awesome, excellent, or fantastic

Try:

(Formal): peerless, stellar, consummate, masterly, magisterial, bravura, pinnacular, summital, surpassing, transcendent, transformative, epochal

(Informal/ vernacular/playful): bone-brilliant, bedazzling, rightful, socko-boffo, trig, legend, raveworthy, pitch-perfect, pukka, pelf, haute, monsta, manna.

(Adventurous): to cark for, superbissimo, tweet-worthy, in the mojo zone, a celestial tantara, a blinder, meta-meta, bung-up-and-bilge-free, *ne plus ultra*, *nulli secundus*, berserkly/heinously great, wizzy, walks on Perrier, *a toda madre*

For: fun (adjective), funny, a ball, a hoot, an upper, happy-making, heartwarming, charming, hilarious

Try:

(Formal): rapturous, blithe, amicable, beatific, ebullient, felicitous, jocund, festal, euphoric, effervescent, infatuating, ludic, comic mayhem

(Informal/vernacular/playful): rousing, larky, frown-flipping, gladsome, a gloomicide, hype, Tiggerish, upful, womby, booyakka, a buster, killing

(Adventurous): cockahooped, shanti for the soul, belly-busting, aneurism-inducingly funny, a brain bacchanalia, cachinnatory, an inoculation of bliss, po-po warming, a pluviosity of joy

For: gorgeous, beautiful, hot, built, great-looking

Try:

(Formal): beguiling, enrapturing, ensorcelling, gracile, transfixing, an objet d'art, lissome, resplendent, Botticellian, Apollonian, idyllic, ravishing

(Informal/vernacular/playful): fetching, ginchy, ga-ga-making, braw, badonkadonked, Junoesque, lavish-limbed, incinerating, peng, smiting, narcotically beautiful, bodilicious, body by Rodin

(Adventurous): arrantly beautiful, swoll, against-the-law handsome, Ava Gardner 2.0, *une belle*, vampirically fetch, wave-the-white-flag beautiful, Denzel Washington 2.0, I've-fallen-and-I-can't-get-up gorgeous

For: great big, huge, gigantic, humongous, lotsa, bunches of
Try:

(Formal): abyssal, avalanchine, cavernous, fathomless, imposing, monumental, planetal, bountiful, a plenitude, mastodonic, oceanic, cataclysmic, chasmal, a nebulosity.

(Informal/vernacular/playful): looming, a lunker, gigabig, crazy large, slathers of, walloping, a goozle, bookoo, hardly a mite, not piddling, fifty-eleven, stonking huge.

(Adventurous): lifty, hippopotamic, a Three Gorges Dam, millioni, a grillion/squillion, pythonic, space-warpingly vast, Burj

Khalifan, Large-Hadron-Collider large, a teravolt or two, from here to the back of the exosphere

For: unbelievable, incredible, mind-blowing, mind-boggling, unreal, beyond belief, indescribable

Try:

(Formal): apparitional, ungluing, dumb-striking, uncanny, startling, bewildering, mind-trammeling, nonplussing, muting, science-fictional, electrifying, phantasmagoric, transmundane

(Informal/vernacular/playful): gobsmacking, flooring, redonkulous, amen-astonishing, skull-spinning, beard-lifting, head-toppling, mind-flummoxing, brain-bludgeoning, clobbers credibility, blindsides belief, hijacks reason, impales logic

(Adventurous): mind-truncheoning, bumfoozling, ontologically out there, a nubilation of unreal, bollixing, pulls your pants off, both-barrels mind-blasting, flooey-making, tongue-stilling, batten-down-the-hatches brain-blowing.

SELECTED SOURCES

AlphaDictionary. Spring 2010. http://www.alphadiction-ary.com/index.shtml

Barrett, Grant, ed. *The Oxford Dictionary of American Political Slang*. New York: Oxford Univ. Press, 2006.

Berrey, Lester V., and Melvin Van Den Bark. *The American Thesaurus of Slang: a Complete Reference Book of Colloquial Speech*. New York: Thomas Crowell, 1942.

Cousineau, Phil. *Wordcatcher: An Odyssey into the World of Weird and Wonderful Words*. Berkeley, Calif.: Viva Editions, 2010.

"Dagree's Great Aussie Slang." Dagree Creations. Spring 2010. http://www.dagree.net/aussieslang/slang_m.html

Dalzell, Tom, and Terry Victor. *The Concise New Partridge Dictionary of Slang and Unconventional English*. London: Routledge, 2008.

Dickson, Paul. *What's in a Name?: Reflections of an Irrepressible Name Collector.* Springfield, Mass.: Merriam-Webster, 1996.

Dictionary and Thesaurus—Free Online at Your Dictionary. Summer 2010. http://www.yourdictionary.com/

"Dictionary of English Slang and Colloquialisms of the UK." Manchester Web Designers. Spring 2010. http://www.peevish.co.uk/slang/

Encyclopedia Britannica Online Encyclopedia. Summer 2010. http://www.britannica.com/

Evans, Ivor H., and Ebenezer Cobham Brewer. *Brewer's Dictionary of Phrase and Fable.* New York: Harper & Row, 1989.

Flexner, Stuart Berg. *Listening to America: An Illustrated History of Words and Phrases from Our Lively and Splendid Past.* New York: Simon and Schuster, 1982.

———, ed. *Random House Webster's Unabridged Dictionary.* 2d Rev. ed. New York: Random House, 2005.

Fowler, H. W., and R. W. Burchfield. *The New Fowler's Modern English Usage.* Oxford: Clarendon, 1996.

Garner, Bryan A. *Garner's Modern American Usage.* Oxford: Oxford Univ. Press, 2003.

Glazier, Stephen. *Random House Word Menu.* New

York: Random House, 1992.

Grambs, David. *The Random House Dictionary for Writers and Readers*. New York: Random House, 1990.

Hughes, Holly. *Best Food Writing 2009*. Philadelphia: Da Capo Lifelong, 2009.

Kay, Christian, ed. *Historical Thesaurus of the Oxford English Dictionary*. Vols. 1–2. New York: Oxford, 2009.

"A Lexicon of Teen Speak." BBC News. Spring 2010. http://news.bbc.co.uk/2/hi/uk_news/magazine/4074004.stm

Lopez, Barry, and Debra Gwartney, eds. *Home Ground: Language for an American Landscape*. San Antonio: Trinity Univ. Press, 2006.

Major, Clarence, ed. *Juba to Jive: a Dictionary of African-American Slang*. New York: Penguin, 1994.

McFedries, Paul. *Word Spy: the Word Lover's Guide to Modern Culture*. New York: Broadway, 2004.

The Meanings and Origins of Sayings and Phrases. Gary Martin. July 2010. http://www.phrases.org.uk/

The Online Slang Dictionary: Real Definitions for Real Slang. Spring 2010. http://onlineslangdictionary.com

The Probert Encyclopedia—Slang. American Veterans Alliance Service Center. Spring 2010. http://vets.com/

questionmanager/encyclopaedia/ency1/PA.HTM

Rap Dictionary. Spring 2010. http://www.rapdict.org

Sherk, Adam. "The Most Overused Buzzwords and Marketing Speak in Press Releases." July 2010. http://adamsherk.com

Speake, Jennifer. *The Oxford Dictionary of Foreign Words and Phrases*. Oxford: Oxford Univ. Press, 1997.

Slang-Dictionary.com—Online Dictionary of Modern Slang. July 2010. http://www.slang-dictionary.com

SlangSite.com—The Slang Dictionary. Summer 2010. http://www.slangsite.com/

Smitherman, Geneva. *Black Talk: Words and Phrases from the Hood to the Amen Corner*. Boston: Houghton Mifflin, 1994.

"Text Message Shorthand." NetLingo, The Internet Dictionary. Spring 2010. http://www.netlingo.com/acronyms.php

"Text Messaging, Chat Abbreviations and Smiley Faces—Webopedia." Webopedia: Online Computer Dictionary for Computer and Internet Terms and Definitions. Spring 2010. http://www.webopedia.com/quick_ref/textmessageabbreviations.asp

Thurner, Dick. *Portmanteau Dictionary: Blend Words in the English Language, including Trademarks and*

Brand Names. Jefferson, N.C.: McFarland & Co., 1993.

Urban Dictionary. Summer 2010. http://www.urbandictionary.com/

Webster's New World Dictionary of Quotations. The Free Dictionary by Farlex. Spring 2010. http://www.thefreedictionary.com/quotes

Wikipedia, the Free Encyclopedia. Spring 2010. http://en.wikipedia.org/wiki/Main_Page

Wordnik: All the Words. Summer 2010. http://www.wordnik.com

ABOUT THE AUTHOR

Arthur Plotnik is a versatile author with a distinguished background in editing and publishing. His seven previous books, two of them Book-of-the-Month Club selections, have been consistently praised for their wit, authority, and exemplary writing. Works on verbal expressiveness include the bestselling *Spunk & Bite: A Writer's Guide to Bold, Contemporary Style*; *The Elements of Expression*; and his new bounty of superlatives, *Better Than Great* (updated news and features at www.freshsuperlatives.com).

A native of White Plains, N.Y., Plotnik studied under Philip Roth in the Iowa Writers Workshop and worked as a staff writer on the Albany (N.Y.) *Times-Union*. He wrote pulp novels for the Scott-Meredith Literary Agency while completing the second of his two master's degrees (English, library service). In Washington he served the Librarian of Congress as press and public relations assistant and newsletter editor. He was later a magazine editor in New York.

With the American Library Association in Chicago, he won numerous honors as editor of *American Libraries* and brought five national awards to ALA's book imprint as editorial director. He was named a charter director of what is now the National Book Awards.

Plotnik, whose *Elements of Editing* is a standard work, has appeared in publications ranging from *Playboy* to *The New York Times*, as well as in a number of literary magazines. A contributor to and board member of *The Writer* magazine, he has written for the *Britannica Book of English Usage* and the "American English" column of *American Way* in-flight magazine. During the Constitution's bicentennial, the National Archives published his award-winning biography of that document's little-known calligrapher.

A biking enthusiast, volunteer tree-steward, and dabbler in jazz piano, he lives in Chicago with his wife, the artist Mary H. Phelan.

INDEX TO SUBCATEGORIES, SPECIAL FEATURES, AND QUOTED AUTHORS

I. Subcategories

Better Than Great is organized into 15 broad categories, each beginning with a short list of subcategories—narrower concepts, as a rule. The combined list below points to the most promising category for the given concept. For example, terms meaning "fast" are found mainly within the category "Forceful." Wider browsing, however, will reward the intrepid word-seeker with additional choices.

II. Special Features

III. Quoted authors

Indexing is to authors (or origins) of the quotations and quoted terms appearing in the lists and introductions. Popular name is used for authors.